For the Love of Renovating

For the Love of Renovating

Tips, Tricks & Inspiration
for Creating Your Dream Home

BARRY BORDELON & JORDAN SLOCUM

UNION
SQUARE
&CO.
NEW YORK

U

UNION
SQUARE
& CO.

NEW YORK

UNION SQUARE & CO. and the distinctive Union Square & Co. logo are
trademarks of Sterling Publishing Co., Inc.

Union Square & Co., LLC, is a subsidiary of Sterling Publishing Co., Inc.

Text © 2024 Barry Bordelon and Jordan Slocum

ISBN 978-1-4549-4927-5 (hardcover)
ISBN 978-1-4549-4928-2 (e-book)

For information about custom editions, special sales, and premium
purchases, please contact specialsales@unionsquareandco.com.

Printed in China

10 9 8 7 6 5 4 3 2 1

unionsquareandco.com

Editor: Caitlin Leffel
Cover and Book Design: Shubhani Sarkar, sarkardesignstudio.com
Art Director: Renée Bollier
Project Editor: Ivy McFadden
Production Manager: Kevin Iwano
Copy Editor: Kathy Brock

See page 288 for photo credits

This book is dedicated to anyone who has the courage to dream of improving their home and then picks up a hammer to get the thing started

Contents

PART I

Getting Started

Introduction

Our homes are so much more than physical spaces. They bring us comfort. They are places where we create memories. They are a way to connect with our families and others when we invite them into our world. They give us a sense of self and the biggest opportunity we have to express ourselves. Naturally, we all dream of having a home or what it could one day be. For many people it takes a lifetime of hard work to have one. So, whether you are buying one, already own one, or even if you're renting, you deserve to create a truly special place to call home.

For us, home is one of the most important things in our lives. We love it—and that's likely because we created every inch of it. We dreamed up each space and then built our dreams. We are deeply connected to it because it contains so much of *us*. That's also why we set out on a journey to help other people build their homes: Because building a home proactively creates memories (you'll be talking about that renovation for years to come, believe us) and can be the ultimate expression of self. It all sounds very cliché, yes, but we understand that when you renovate a home, you're putting a lot of yourself into it. Not to mention spending all of your money, so you should love it!

Think about your kitchen: Obviously, you need a stove and a fridge, but that's not what most of our clients say when they describe the kitchen of their dreams, and it's not what we first thought about when we set out to build ours. We wanted our kitchen to be a social place. A gathering place for us, our friends, and our family to enjoy each other's company and to connect. That's the first thing our clients say too. Only after that do we talk about the stove and the fridge.

After dreaming and saving for years, we were finally able to purchase our first home together. We knew that we couldn't afford to buy a home that was move-in ready, and truth be told, we didn't want to! We desperately wanted to pour our heart, soul, blood, and tears into creating a place that would truly be our home. So that's our first piece of advice: Before you start picking tile and paint colors, spend a few minutes thinking about what you want your home to mean to you.

So that leads us to why you're reading this book. You're setting out on the journey of a lifetime to create what could possibly be the most important thing in your life: your home. You've got to get it right, but you've never done it before (or maybe just once), so how in the wild world are you going to do it? Seriously. The details. You need them. And we're going to give them to you.

Is it scary? Yes. Is it fun? Yes. Is it rewarding? Absolutely. Will you do it again? You'll definitely tell yourself you won't (but you might). But buckle up, because we're going for a ride. Bring a pencil and a whole lot of Post-its to mark some pages. We sincerely know that we can help you create a home you'll love.

About Us

We didn't intend to become the go-to renovation team for historic Brooklyn brownstones. We weren't setting out to be featured in design publications or even on renovation TV shows. We had no idea that we would have fans around the world looking to us not only for inspiration but also to help them figure out how to renovate their kitchens and bathrooms. We didn't know we would hold so many people's hands through buying a fixer-upper, understanding the process and costs, and designing and building their homes. But here we are, and we're now hungry to share more.

We both had experience in real estate and design in different ways. Barry dreamed of being an architect and even made it halfway through architecture school before life had other plans for him. Instead, he found a passion for real estate, and after buying his first small one-bedroom apartment, he renovated and sold it. After doing that a few more times over a decade, he figured out how to design and build a space other people would enjoy. Jordan has always been creative, attending film school and then becoming a baker, which led him to helping design and build bakeries and ice cream shops. But even that experience didn't give us a clue for what was to come.

We started our home-building journey together several years ago when we bought our beat-up old (1890) Brooklyn brownstone. She had been carved up into so many different versions of a home over the years that there were (and still are) scars to show for it. By that point, we had spent nearly a year looking for the right home to restore and had developed a deeper understanding of what we wanted. We had bounced around from house to house in the sweltering New York summer, battling crowds at open houses and feeling the pressure to compete for each one. When we walked into the place that would become our home, we saw past the layers of paint, decaying plaster, and carved-up layout and had no doubt that this was the house for us. We were thrilled to restore her to her former glory as a loved home.

As we planned our renovation, we noticed that there was a lack of information about restoring and renovating an old house. This was unlike any other project we have ever taken on in both scope and scale, and we knew we needed help. Some of the best advice we were able to find was on other creative blogs, so we decided to share our experiences as well, and that's how the *Brownstone Boys* blog came to be. Shortly after the launch, we were asked to write for Brownstoner.com, where we still contribute a regular series. Since then, our blog and social media have become a resource for anyone who is embarking on a renovation journey of their own.

Eventually some people who reached out to us seemed to really need help with their renovation projects. We thought hard about it and worked up the courage to ask someone, "Would you like us to help you with it?" and just like that we had our first client. That quickly led to a second, then a third, and eventually we knew it was time to quit our day jobs. We have been so fortunate to be able to inspire others to tackle renovation and restoration projects big and small, and we pinch ourselves every day that it is now our career.

Fast-forward to today, and we have gone from first-time historic home renovators desperately seeking any info on how to do it to not only providing that info for others but also helping dozens of young families design and build their dream homes. We love creating beautiful spaces! And we love finding ways to renovate on a budget! Most of all, we are thrilled to help people create something as important as their home. That's why we decided to write this book: not only to inspire you to tackle design and renovation projects big and small but also to hold your hand as you do it.

Getting Started

The dreamy dark
tones in the sofa
and woodwork are
contrasted with
plenty of natural light
from the windows.
Two antique mirrors
add depth and make
this cozy room feel
spacious.

Buying a Fixer-Upper

Our living room didn't always look this open or bright, but with a fixer-upper, you can unveil and elevate existing features, like the original wood window and door moulding.

T he rest of the chapters in this book will walk you through designing and renovating every part of your home. But we are dedicating this first chapter to those of you who are interested in or intent on buying a fixer-upper.

Most of our clients reach out to us when they decide that the only way to create a home that's truly theirs—exactly what they want in every way—while still keeping everything in budget is to find a house that needs love. (Sometimes tough love.) So we thought we would start here. If you are spending your weekends scouring the real estate listings and looking at houses that need their fair share of attention, then you might have found that choosing the right one to renovate is just as important as how you renovate it. How do you know if a house can be your dream home when it's finished? How much work is too much? Is the purchase price plus the cost of the renovation in your budget? Which professionals should you bring to look at the house for an opinion on scope and cost? We find that most people have a lot of questions about the process, and one of the biggest is whether they should renovate or buy a move-in-ready home. Let's take each question one at a time.

Older homes can have so much character. Even in this one shot, you'll see historic woodwork, wall accents, an original stair post, and antique vent grates.

Should you buy a fixer-upper and pour your heart and soul into a renovation—or just buy a move-in-ready home?

That's the big question, but we'll make it easy for you. If you bought this book and are reading this now, then you should probably renovate! Some people have the desire to create something that they can call their own. They care greatly about all the details, and they want to take part in the process. If that's you (heck, you already bought a book about it!), then you might not ever be satisfied with all of the details someone else chose, possibly years ago, or even worse for some of us, things a developer chose! (Scream and wince here.)

As we're sure you already know, there is a whole lot more to it! Yes, creating your own home can be one of the most meaningful things you'll do in your life, and you'll tell stories (good and bad) for years, but there will be stress and anxiety and as many low points as high points along the way, so you should know what you are getting into.

Overall the most important thing is that you have to be motivated to do it. You need to have at least a little bit of a burning desire to create this masterpiece you've been dreaming of. Just like anything that takes time and is hard, to go through the entire process you must want to do it! And that brings us back to the fact that you picked up this book. So congrats on taking a very big step in what will be an exciting journey!

In this fixer-upper, we focused on the core elements of this original room: natural light and a beautiful fireplace, to envision how we could renovate the space.

Before

After

Here, we have two different tones in the original woodwork, providing a subtle contrast. When restoring them we left them that way to emphasize the detail in both designs.

Pros and Cons of Buying a Fixer-Upper

THE GOOD

- Customizing every fixture, finish, and detail in your home.

- Having a home that truly reflects who you are.

- Having a very special connection to your home as you'll be intimately familiar with every detail, with stories to tell about how it got to where it is.

- Potentially getting a much nicer house: bigger, better, preferred location, and more custom at a lower cost.

- Creating a layout that's cohesive with your lifestyle.

- Experiencing the once-in-a-lifetime opportunity to renovate a house. (But never say never! You may want to do it again.)

- Creating value in your home that you can use in several ways, such as reselling it for a profit, pulling out equity, or creating a family heirloom to pass down to the generations!

THE BAD

- It can be a stressful experience dealing with surprises, working with contractors, ordering materials, and making mistakes along the way.

- It will be months before you can move in—or, if you choose to move in during the renovation, you'll be living in a construction site.

- It can be time-consuming going through the process of building the design, choosing the finishes, working with the construction crews, and troubleshooting along the way.

- You have to be up for surprises, twists, and turns, many of which are expensive and time-consuming.

- You will likely need to make compromises.

How do you know if a house can be your dream home when it's finished?

What you view as your dream home is up to you! It's *your* dream. It can be overwhelming comparing properties. Each will have pros and cons. None of the houses you see will tick every box. The trick is to find the one that ticks the most boxes of *your* top priorities. So make a list! Here is a list of ten potential priorities, in no particular order because it's up to you to sort them or to add others to the list.

1. A preferred neighborhood

2. Walking distance to restaurants, cafes, and bars

3. Outdoor space

4. Historic original features

5. Amount of square footage (if you're not open to adding on)

6. Type of house (brick, wood, brownstone, etc.)

7. Style of house (historic, Victorian, craftsman, ranch, Cape Cod, bungalow, modern, etc.)

8. Number of bedrooms and/or bathrooms (unless you have enough square footage to add additional rooms, or you're up for building on to the home)

9. Scope of project. Some houses are huge projects, others need a lighter touch. Are you okay tackling a huge one, or would you rather just do some cosmetic upgrades and move in?

10. Budget. The larger and more expensive the renovation, the lower the purchase price will need to be.

There are so many more possibilities, so you should also think hard about the top priority or priorities specific to you. For instance, we wanted a historic Brooklyn brownstone. There are a lot of houses around that are not brownstones, but it's been our dream to restore one for years. So that was our priority, and everything else moved down in the list.

The last two items on the list above are big ones. So let's now talk more about those.

This old junk shop was a former carriage house! We had to stretch our imagination to rethink this entire property. See how it turned out on pages 200–201.

HOW MUCH WORK IS TOO MUCH?

This goes hand in hand with the next question. The three factors you need to consider when evaluating the scope of a project are money, time, and motivation.

1. Money. First, consider what your all-in budget is, then think about how much of that budget you want or are willing to spend on renovation. If you look at a house that's close to the top of your budget and it needs a total gut renovation, it might not be the house for you. If you see a house that's perfect except for the kitchen and it's close to the top of your budget, it might be a contender. The bigger the renovation is, the more money you'll need to reserve, which requires a lower purchase price.

2. Time. One of the things you need to think about is how much time you are willing to wait before moving in or, if you are planning on renovating while living there (may the force be with you), how long you are willing to live in a construction site. The bigger the project, the longer it will take. Many people spend a year working on a full gut renovation, while the cosmetic upgrade to a kitchen as mentioned above might be only a couple of months and easier (yet still inconvenient) to live through.

3. Motivation. Renovating a house can be a lot of fun! We love it and can't get enough. You might even find your inner designer along the way, as we did. But you have to be prepared for twists, turns, ups, downs, lows, and highs. We always tell our clients it is a rollercoaster ride. There are moments of excitement, moments of despair, moments of relief, and moments of joy. You'll cry. You'll laugh. You might beat your head against a wall. Daily. So consider how much you are up for it emotionally!

What are the factors that tell you how big a project is? When we initially look at a house, one of the first things we notice is not necessarily how awful it might look but rather how close the configuration is to what we want. If the kitchen is in the wrong place, walls need to move, bathrooms relocated, bedrooms reconfigured, and we have a full gut renovation on our hands no matter how good or bad the house looks. That many configuration changes will likely require almost all new plumbing, electrical, flooring, and other details. If all of the rooms are in the right places, then we'll look at the condition of the flooring, electrical, plumbing, and plaster.

We work mostly in historical homes built in the late 1800s; many times even if the original floors are in decent shape, years of settling have caused them to slant in every direction. That immediately tells us that not only do these floors need to come up so that we can level everything, install new subfloor, and put in new flooring, but also there will be a lot of fallout from that work. For instance, much if not all of the trim and doors will need to be replaced or removed and reinstalled (as the height of the floors is adjusted). It's a big job. (See chapter 9.)

Plumbing, electrical, and HVAC (heating, ventilation, and air-conditioning) are your other big-ticket items. Look at the main electrical panel. Does it look older than about fifteen years? If so, there have likely been dozens of electrical code upgrades since, and when an electrician starts doing any work, everything will need to be brought up to code. Even if the electrical has been upgraded, it is likely a hodgepodge of old and new and won't fly when inspected. Also, almost none of our projects have air-conditioning built into the home. So we know HVAC will need to be added, and—surprise—integrating that into an old home comes with a lot of additional electrical, plumbing, and building work.

IS THE PURCHASE PRICE PLUS THE COST OF THE RENOVATION IN YOUR BUDGET?

We have already started to discuss this. It's a sliding scale. What is your all-in budget? Basically how much do you have to spend even if you stretch yourself to your max? The closer the asking price (or what you feel it will sell for . . . it could be higher or lower) of the house is to your all-in budget, the less you'll have for renovations. Hopefully, houses that need more work will be priced less. So that leads us to a very important thing to note: Watch out for the "lipstick on a pig" out there. Savvy real estate agents can come in and clean things up enough to fool the average buyer into getting a better impression of the home than they should. Fresh paint on the walls could be hiding cracking plaster, clever staging with beautiful furniture can distract you from the condition of the house, new light fixtures might make you feel like it has an updated electrical system, and cleaned-up mechanicals (boiler, hot water heater) might disguise their age, but in reality the home needs all new mechanicals, a full electrical upgrade, extensive plaster repairs, walls and rooms relocated, new floors, a new roof, and a brand-new kitchen and bathrooms. Many buyers walk into those spaces and feel much better about it versus the house they just saw that has old, gross carpet that smells like cat pee, peeling paint, and decaying mechanicals. But both of these homes could need the same amount of work to transform them into your dream home; there is no cost savings during the renovation for the cleaner house when that much work needs to be done. If they are charging more for it, then you might do better with the uglier, smellier one and the lower price tag. It can be tough to spot these "lipstick on a pig" houses, but if we see fresh paint in a house that obviously needs a *ton* of work, light fixtures that don't seem like they belong, or other signs of quick upgrades, we should ask some questions about any recently done work.

One of our most memorable examples of this is a house we saw that had a very freshly painted cellar floor. It was so spotless we felt like we needed to take our shoes off to walk on it, while the rest of the house hadn't been touched in years. It turns out they did a quick paint job before the open house and were hiding a very bad flooding issue that had been a consistent problem.

So we are sure you're still wondering, "How do I know how much the renovation will cost?!" We've got you in the next chapter!

While we were a bit terrified of the stained, crumbling floor, we were mesmerized by the stunning skylight in this old carriage house.

Who should you bring with you to view the property?

For our clients, us! We often look at potential fixer-uppers with our clients to determine the cost and scope of a property. But if we're not available, you can also bring a local architect or general contractor. There are even design-build firms that do it all! But you probably won't be able to enlist any of these folks to come around and look at every house with you, so you'll need to do a first pass on your own to try to understand the scope and cost of the work, which is what we'll help you with in the next chapter. If you determine that the home is indeed a possibility, then you can go back to a second showing with the professional of your choice. We recommend choosing that person so they're ready to go, because real estate markets can be competitive, and securing the home may happen very quickly.

THINK OUTSIDE THE BOX

This can be fun! There may be properties out there that at first glance look like they might not be contenders, but if you keep an open mind, you could find something that can be more uniquely yours than you ever thought possible. What might look too small could potentially be made bigger (depending on local building ordinances); what is ugly can be made beautiful; what is decaying can be restored, heck . . . you can even tear the place down and start over!

You might even be able to find a home that needs love and is not on the market. If you see a house that looks vacant in a neighborhood you are targeting and you think it has potential, pull over and explore. If you're brave enough, knock on a neighbor's door and ask them if they know who owns it. Or just get the address and look it up in your city's property records. You may be able to get a hold of the owner, who might take you up on your offer to buy it. If you are able to find a house that's not on the market, you'll have less (or no) competition from other buyers, and you can avoid brokers' fees.

Finally—don't forget to have fun out there! Shopping for a house to renovate can seem overwhelming, but the good news is that, in theory, anything is possible. You can cosmetically upgrade kitchens and bathrooms. You can add rooms or floors to a house. You can redo all of the mechanicals. You can add air-conditioning. You can excavate the cellar to create more living spaces. You can create a roof deck. You can blow a huge hole in the back of the house and put in a moving glass wall to have the indoor/outdoor lifestyle of your dreams. Anything can be done; it just all depends on your budget and how long you are willing to wait to realize the result. Maybe it's because we are totally comfortable embarking on a full gut renovation, but we would be inclined to get the house in the worst condition at the lowest cost so that we can put in all of the features we want.

Budget Breakdown

When it comes to house shopping, the best way to keep the budget in check is to know where you are willing to make some compromises. If you aren't willing to make any compromises, then you'll pay top dollar for your house. If it has to be in the best neighborhood, in perfect shape, and move-in ready, and it ticks all the boxes and then some, chances are lots of other people think the same thing, as well as the sellers. On the other hand, if you're willing to find a place that needs love (perhaps a lot), is not quite in the perfect neighborhood, and will take some time to make it beautiful, then you will get more house for less money. Here are our top compromises to consider to keep the purchase price of your house down:

- Look for a house that needs work. You've probably heard about getting the ugliest house in the best neighborhood.

- Look for a house that's perhaps just outside of your target neighborhood or in a completely different one that might have the potential to be your new favorite.

- Be willing to wait to get the house of your dreams. It might not be move-in ready, but in a few quick months or even a year, it can be the perfect house.

- Consider buying a house that might be too small but can be added on to.

- Keep an open mind that anything can be changed, from the layout, the facade and curb appeal, the square footage, and, of course, all the fixtures and finishes.

Recipe for Buying a Fixer-Upper

1. Make a list of your priorities and rank them in order from highest to lowest.

2. Search listings, find an agent who has done or specializes in hunting for fixer-uppers, and keep an eye out for properties that are not on the market.

3. Look at the house to assess if it has potential to meet your top priorities, remembering that it may not fulfill every one of them. As long as it satisfies the most important ones (or has the potential to), it could be a contender.

4. Try to get an understanding of scope and cost of the work that you want to do (see chapter 2 for more information on budgeting).

5. Look out for "lipstick on a pig" listings and try to understand the amount of work a house really needs to help you decide whether one in slightly better condition with a higher price tag is worth it.

6. Analyze the cost of the renovation along with what you anticipate being the sales cost to see if it meets your all-in budget.

7. Look at comparable homes that have recently sold in the area to make sure that your purchase cost plus renovation budget isn't drastically more than what it could potentially sell for.

8. If your analysis confirms that the home could work for you, schedule a second showing with a professional (architect, general contractor, designer, or design-build firm—or a Brownstone Boy!) to confirm your general cost estimate.

9. Make an offer and buy a house!

What You'll Need

- Patience!
- Chapter 2 of this book to help you estimate the renovation cost
- An architect, general contractor, designer, or design-build professional on hand
- That list of your priorities
- A calculator and phone/camera to take pictures and videos of the houses you view so that you remember the condition and details

Let the Renovation Begin

It's all about the
juxtaposition of
black and white in
this vestibule and
entryway–crisp,
modern, and elegant.

W e talk to people all the time who have found their fixer-upper or decided to renovate their existing space—and get completely stuck on what to do next. For some, it's because it seems like there are so many daunting tasks ahead that it's hard to know where to start! But it's also because, inevitably, this is the time to really start thinking about the B-word: *budget*. If your blood pressure just shot up a bit—we get it. But we're here to help you remain calm and keep your eyes on the prize: the joy of designing and renovating your home.

Formerly a dark, damp space, this carriage house kitchen is now full of modern lines, functional storage, and gorgeous light.

Determining Your Reasonably Comfortable Budget

Our style is very historic charm-meets-modern design, so we love adding unconventional shapes and stark lines—like these chairs and built-in shelves—in old homes.

The first step, before you start talking to professionals (architects, designers, contractors), is getting a handle on what you are *reasonably comfortable* spending on your project. *Reasonably* because you want to make sure your scope of work isn't unreasonable for your budget (or vice versa), and *comfortable* because you want to make sure you can afford everything, including hard costs (construction labor, materials, finishes) and soft costs (architecture, city filings, carrying costs, alternative accommodations). If you bought a fixer-upper, you've likely given this some thought, but if you are starting to consider renovating a home you already own, this might be the first time you attach your dollars to your dream.

Our first piece of advice is to develop a budget early. It might be tempting to wait until the architect or contractor comes in, but we've seen a lot of people end up with a beautiful design from an architect they can't afford to build, or they just don't know what range they should expect when quotes come back from a contractor. Knowing what your reasonably comfortable budget is before you approach the professionals can help steer the ship so you aren't left with a design you can't afford or entertaining inflated quotes from a contractor to someone who hasn't thought about how much the project should cost.

BUDGETING TECHNIQUES

There are a few ways to develop your budget. And as you have probably realized, there is a wide range of costs, depending on the scope of work and what types of finishes you choose. Many of those details are likely not worked out at this point, so you can figure out your reasonably comfortable initial budget now, understanding it might be adjusted later. That way it can help inform the design process, too, and keep the scope of work realistic. We recommend a different technique to estimate costs on a total home renovation versus just a single room project. Let's look at how to develop your reasonably comfortable initial budget so that you can move on to other steps. Then, as we go through each room of your house, the budget can become more refined.

Terms to Know

- **Hard Costs:** The actual costs to build your home, including labor and construction materials as well as fixtures and finishes.

- **Soft Costs:** The costs from architects, designers, engineers, as well as city filing fees.

- **Carrying Costs:** The amount you might need to spend on the home while you aren't living there. This can include utilities, taxes, HOA (homeowners association) fees, insurance, and expenses for alternative accommodations if you can't live in the home while you are renovating.

- **Price per Square Foot:** The costs of the renovation divided by the square footage of the home. This can help you get a better picture of the general cost of the project.

- **Contingency:** The amount you reserve above and beyond the hard and soft costs of the project for unforeseen expenses.

TOTAL HOME RENOVATION

This type of renovation is big and all encompassing. Since a lot of things go into a big project, you need a quick way to estimate costs, and one of the quickest ways to get a general idea of budget is to use a price per square foot and apply it to the square footage of your home. If you bought a home that needs a gut renovation, or close to it, this can provide a general rule of thumb to figure out the costs. This technique does have a few flaws. First, it doesn't get specific enough to pinpoint the costs for renovating a room. For instance, a kitchen will have a higher price per square foot to renovate than a bedroom, simply because there's a lot more expensive stuff that goes into a kitchen than a bedroom. A price per square foot for the entire house will give you a general idea of the total cost for a renovation, taking into account that there is a kitchen, a few bedrooms, and several bathrooms. So, although it's not a bad way to generalize the cost of a complete home renovation, it's not a good way to evaluate costs by room, because you can't take that number and apply it just to a kitchen (that would be higher) or just to a bedroom (that would be lower). Also, there may be a feature of your renovation that could push the costs up outside the price per square foot, such as adding an addition to a home, which comes with many more costs than renovating within the home's footprint. You'll want to treat these big special features as separate line items.

Before we get to the numbers, you should know that we do renovations in New York City, so the numbers we work with are more in line with renovating in big cities. Those are on the high end, but we've provided a range so that you can adjust down if you live in a place with a lower cost of living. Note that this is true for contractor and labor expenses, but costs for finish items would likely be the same, since many suppliers are national.

PRICE PER SQUARE FOOT (PSF) BUDGETING FOR A TOTAL HOME RENOVATION	
Budget-conscious reno with low-cost finishes and little to no structural work	$125 to $175 psf
Mid-range reno with mostly basic finishes, some upgrades, and some structural work	$175 to $200 psf
Mid-range reno with nice finishes, some splurges, and structural work	$200 to $300 psf
High-end renovation with structural work, high-end finishes	$300 to $450 psf
Super high-end renovation with a well-known architect, designer, and all high-end, best-of-class finishes	$450+ psf

Hopefully you can find yourself in one of these brackets so you can generalize the cost of renovating your recently purchased fixer-upper or existing home! Now, that gives you the hard costs of the renovation, but there are other expenses you should take into consideration as well. Depending on the size of your project (more on that coming up on page 44), you might need an architect, engineers, and city filings. And remember that if it's a larger project and you won't be living in the home during the process, you'll want to include carrying costs like the mortgage, insurance, utility bills, and possibly alternative accommodations while the work is being done.

Finally, don't forget to include a contingency budget of 10 to 15 percent of the total renovation cost. There are almost always additional expenses that come up during the renovation. Once walls, floors, and ceilings are opened up, it's quite possible some repairs may be needed that were not visible before. You also may have to or want to alter a design to account for conditions on-site. These items are called *change orders*. They can be stressful, so if you have a budget allotted for them, it can make the process much smoother.

Here is an example of a budget for a 2,400-square-foot house with mid-range finishes and some splurges:

HARD COSTS	
Construction labor and materials + finish items @ $250 psf	$600,000
SOFT COSTS	
Architecture and engineering	$35,000
Carrying costs (e.g., mortgage, property taxes, HOA fees, and utilities)	$24,000
Alternative accommodations	$18,000
TOTAL COSTS	**$677,000**
Contingency (10%)	$67,700
FINAL TOTAL	**$744,700**

APARTMENT RENOVATION

If you're renovating an apartment, the costs should be less because you are only working on your unit. The general electrical, plumbing, roof, and so on for the building is the responsibility of the condo or cooperative association, and you would pay only for alterations within your unit. You will likely have less flexibility to make major layout and structural changes. On the plus side, it can also keep the costs down!

APARTMENT RENOVATION PRICE PER SQUARE FOOT	
Budget-conscious reno with low-cost finishes	$75 to $125 psf
Mid-range reno with mostly basic finishes and some upgrades	$125 to $175 psf
Mid-range reno with upgraded finishes and some splurges	$175 to $225 psf
High-end renovation with high-end finishes	$225 to $300 psf
Super high-end renovation with a well-known architect, designer, and all high-end, best-of-class finishes	$300+ psf

Here is an example of a 1,000-square-foot apartment renovation budget with mostly basic finishes and some upgrades:

HARD COSTS	
Construction labor and materials + finish items @$150 psf	$150,000
SOFT COSTS	
Architecture and engineering	$22,000
Carrying costs (e.g., mortgage, property taxes, HOA fees, utilities)	$12,000
Alternative accommodations	$10,000
TOTAL	$194,000
Contingency (10%)	$19,400
FINAL TOTAL	$213,400

SINGLE-ROOM RENOVATIONS

If you're taking on a renovation of just a single room, it's easier to figure out the cost directly. Since the scope is more limited, you can put the numbers for hard and soft costs together and come up with a lump-sum budget.

KITCHEN	
Budget	$20,000 to $30,000
Mid-grade	$30,000 to $45,000
High-end	$50,000+
BATHROOM	
Budget	$15,000 to $25,000
Mid-grade	$25,000 to $30,000
High-end	$35,000 to $50,000+
LIVING ROOM	
Budget	$5,000 to $8,000
Mid-grade	$8,000 to $15,000
High-end	$15,000 to $20,000+
BEDROOM	
Budget	$5,000 to $10,000
Mid-grade	$10,000 to $15,000
High-end	$15,000 to $25,000+

DETAILED BUDGET

The true cost of your renovation won't be known until you get quotes from contractors and have all of your finish materials specified and quoted. This will be your detailed budget, and that usually doesn't happen until after an architect draws up the plans and puts together a "bid set" of drawings that the contractor will use to produce a quote. Perfect segue.

WHAT HAPPENS IF YOUR DETAILED BUDGET COMES IN TOO HIGH?

Hopefully the reasonably comfortable initial budget you worked so hard putting together (see page 34) informed your project scope as you went through the design process, but if it didn't, what do you do? You have two options. You can reduce the scope of your project (aka make compromises), or you can find more money to fund your project. Maybe there are some areas of your project that you already have earmarked as "nice-to-haves." Look at the cost of some of those items, prioritize what is most important to you, and find some things to cut. Alternatively, if you aren't willing to compromise on any, you can look into funding options to finance some or even all of your project (see "Financing Your Renovation," opposite).

The subtle star of this hallway is the sliding glass pocket door. We love that it provides privacy and a sound barrier without cutting off the light coming in the study window.

Financing Your Renovation

If you don't have the money ready and waiting in your bank account for your project, that doesn't mean it's impossible. Renovating your home will add value, and banks know it. Many of them are willing to give you a loan on the future value of your home. We have many clients who use this option. Here are some loans that you should be aware of:

Construction Loan: A construction loan is similar to a mortgage but is based on an assessed value post-construction. The bank will need a lot of documents from you regarding the renovation so that they can come up with that assessment. They will want to see architectural plans, a fully executed contract with the builder, a construction schedule, and a schedule of payments. They typically disperse the funds to you throughout the project based on that schedule of payments.

Home Equity Loan (HELOAN): A home equity loan is based on the equity you have in your home. So, if your home is assessed at $200,000 and you owe $150,000, you can borrow on the $50,000 of equity you have. Some banks will even consider the post-construction value, which will give you much more equity to borrow against. These require similar documents as a construction loan, but they will usually disburse all of the funds in one payment.

Home Equity Line of Credit (HELOC): A bank offers a home equity line of credit based on the equity you have in your home (similar to the HELOAN), but instead you get a line of credit to pay for your renovation. You might be able to base the assessment on the post-construction value.

FOLLOWING PAGE:

This parlor is balanced between modern, elegant, and historic features. The ornate marble fireplace and the original mirror are complemented by the simplicity of the sofas.

Assembling the Team

Now that the reasonably comfortable initial budget has become more detailed, you can take the big step of starting to assemble your renovation team. Choosing the team is one of the most important things you'll do. You're going to spend countless hours with them as your home is designed and built. Now, you may have heard to get three quotes for everything. Three quotes are good, but five (or more!) are even better. Ten anyone? We promise you won't regret spending extra time looking for a quality team and thoroughly vetting them. If a contractor is difficult, slow, and unresponsive in the quoting process—the time when you would expect them to put their best foot forward—you can bet they will be worse once you're in the thick of it. Make sure you feel good about how you can work with them, because there will be problems to solve, details to work out, negotiations, and likely a few tense moments. One of the best ways to find good people is to ask around. Do you know someone who did a renovation similar to yours, with a similar budget and good results? Ask them if they would recommend their architect or contractor. You may also find online listings and resources for your area with ratings.

The first question you may be wondering is who exactly you need. We'll talk about a bunch of different players, but you may not need them all. If your project is a basic cosmetic remodel of, let's say, a bathroom or a kitchen and you aren't moving plumbing or gas lines or shifting walls, then you might not need an architect. You would just need a contractor to do the work. You may want a designer to help with the finish materials, or you may decide that you can handle that yourself. If you are gutting a house, moving walls, or putting a bathroom or a kitchen where there wasn't one previously, then you will likely want an architect and engineers (whom the architect will bring in). In any case, be sure to ask about the permit requirements in your area. They are the experts and will be able to help.

ARCHITECT

If your project is of a size that requires it, the architect is likely the first member of the team you'll want on board. They can also provide a lot of resources for you throughout the process. We recommend considering three to five architects who might be a good fit and setting up a meeting with each to view the house. Walk them through and explain all of your hopes and dreams for the space. Hear what they have to say, and see if it aligns with your vision. Ask them to explain their process from beginning to end, what types of renderings and elevations of spaces (see page 45) they intend to produce, what drawings they will provide, and how involved they will be in the construction process. Look at their previous work on their website or social media. Have they done similar types of projects in a style that aligns with your vision of the space?

Get a proposal from any of them whom you are interested in working with. You might find that they each charge for services a bit differently. Some architects charge a fixed fee for their work but include line items for different phases and expenses like engineering. Others may charge a percentage of the costs of the project (including finishes, if they source them). They can be hard to compare, so we recommend coming up with a total cost for each architect you're considering and using that. When the architect has seen the house, understands the scope of work, and delivers the proposal, you can ask them for their estimation on what the project will cost. See if it aligns with your reasonably comfortable initial budget (see page 34), and don't forget that those soft costs, like the architectural fees, need to fit into it too.

Once you choose an architect and sign a contract, usually the first thing they will do is schedule a time to go back to the house to thoroughly measure it. After that they will move to the schematic design process. A few weeks after measuring, they will produce several options with different floor plans, elevations, and renderings of the space. They will present these to you so that you

What Plans Will You Need for Your Renovation?

You'll definitely want to make sure you have the proper drawings for your contractor to follow. The most common types of drawings are plan views and elevation views. Plan views are bird's-eye views that look down on the house; they can tell a lot of the story but not everything since there are a lot of details on the walls. For instance, you can look at a plan view of a bathroom and see where the sink, toilet, and tub are located, but you can't see how high the vanity sconce should be mounted, how high above the counter the outlet should be installed, or where the wall tile will go. Elevation views show the walls of the rooms, so they will illustrate all the details you can't see from the plan views. Your contractor will need both for at least some areas. We would recommend at least having some elevations of the kitchen, bathrooms, and any architecturally significant areas of the home.

Once the details are worked out, the architect will file your plans with the municipality for approval. Depending on where you live, this process can take several weeks. Once the project has approval, the contractor can pull the permits and begin.

can either choose which versions of the space you like or provide feedback for them to redesign. A week or two later they will present the final schematic design based on your feedback. If your architect is choosing some finish material for you, they may also present that around this time. When the schematic design is finalized, they can then start working on the "bid set" (the set of drawings used to provide to contractors for bidding) and/or a final set of drawings that will be filed with your city or municipality. (The final set of drawings can also be used for the contractor to bid on.)

INTERIOR DESIGNER

You are about to embark on a journey to transform a house into your new home. You probably have lots of inspiration pictures, Pinterest pins, and ideas of what you want your space to look like. Now comes the fun (and hard) part: making those inspiration pictures come to life! You may choose to go it alone and do your own design and choose all of your own finishes. You certainly can, and in chapter 3 and throughout the book, we will teach you a lot of skills to help you undertake this successfully. It can be very rewarding and, who knows, it might even develop into a career for you (ahem!). But it's not easy, and it's incredibly time-consuming. Be prepared to have some head-scratching moments, and plan on reordering and replanning multiple times as you go through the learning process. If that kind of challenge isn't something you are up to, then you may choose to hire an interior designer. An interior designer will listen to your vision of the space and piece everything together for you. They will use your inspiration and tastes, add their own to it, and produce something that is you—and then some.

Note that sometimes your architect can also act as an interior designer (for an additional fee, of course). Also, if your project doesn't require an architect, you can still hire an interior designer to produce the drawings and elevation your contractor will need.

CONTRACTOR

Now that you have a set of architectural plans and a design, you have something to give contractors to bid on the project. Usually they will need to see some type of drawings to provide a bid. The drawings will tell them how many walls are being demolished, how many new walls are being built, where the plumbing and electrical are being run, where the tiling, cabinets, and stone are going, and many other details. If your project is small, like just a kitchen or bathroom renovation, and you aren't using an architect or an interior designer, you might be able to put together a bullet-pointed "scope of work" to communicate all of the details.

Our biggest challenge with this loft kitchen was creating more space. We moved the entry door over to gain 3 valuable feet of kitchen space.

Before

After

Choosing the right contractor is one of the most important things you can do to set up your project for success (no pressure!). If you know anyone who has been through a similar renovation, that's a great place to start asking for recommendations. If you happen to see another reno project in your neighborhood, get their contractor's name or look for a sign. Of course, there is also always the internet. If you are using an architect or interior designer, they will no doubt have recommendations as well. Once you have a list of three to five potential contractors, send them your drawings and elevations and schedule a walk-through of the space with each of the candidates. It might be a bit time-consuming, but the time you spend with them at this point is when you will get a lot of information about how it will be to work with them through a long and detailed process with a lot of ups and a lot of downs. (If your project is a smaller one, it might be possible to just walk the contractor through, provide a basic scope of work, and explain what you want to do.)

As you walk through each room, talk about what you want to do and listen to their thoughts and comments. Do they sound collaborative? Do they have ideas? Do they seem knowledgeable about the work? Or do they just tell you every reason you shouldn't do something? You want to make sure the person seems like someone you can work with closely day in and day out to make your vision come to life. One of the things we like to hear is that they have done similar types of projects. Listen for things such as "Yes, in another project we built a similar kitchen with a large picture window overlooking the yard, and it was beautiful." Or "In a previous job, when we opened up the floor, we found joists that were cracked and needed to be replaced." The contractor will be your primary problem-solving partner, so you want to make sure they are up for the challenge.

Now, one of the most important moments in the process of assembling your team: the contractor quote. Every renovation is a careful balance of the scope and the budget. Unfortunately, money is an object. So this is an area when you need to thread a very important needle. You want to make sure you are getting the most scope of work done and that the contractor you go with is reputable, knowledgeable, and competent. There are contractors who may offer a lower price, but they may not be able to provide the finish level you expect. Or there may be amazing and talented contractors who are priced high for very good reasons but the cost is too high to get all of the work done. Finding someone who is a balance of both can be difficult, so just like when choosing the rest of your team, you should get as many quotes as possible. You may have also heard that you shouldn't go with the lowest bid. That may not always be true, but it usually is. At the very least, if a contractor provides a bid that is an outlier, either too high or too low, you will want to understand why. So ask questions.

Looking at contractor quotes side by side might be frustrating. You'll find that they all use different methods to format their quotes. They may lump things together or not provide detail in some areas. One thing you can do to hopefully help standardize quotes is provide a template they can fill out. Warning: Putting

Questions to Ask Your Contractor

- What similar projects have you done?
- How long do you think the project will take?
- When are you available to start?
- What obstacles or issues do you foresee?
- How often will you be on-site?
- Will you have a foreman present when you are not on-site?
- How often will we meet on-site?
- How long will the project take?
- Can you provide references?
- How many jobs do you currently have? Do you have the capacity for my job?

together a quote can be time-consuming for them, so they may or may not agree to use a template.

You will likely see big variations in line items between contractors. That's normal. Some contractors have people on staff who do certain things while others subcontract work out. If you find, say, one electrical line item is much higher than others, you might want to ask some questions and see if they can possibly get a quote from another subcontractor.

Once you've narrowed your options to two or three contractors, carefully examine the quotes side by side. Make sure all of your questions are answered. Possibly schedule a second walk-through or meeting with them to discuss the project further. Once you choose one contractor, make sure you understand when they are available to start and what their expected completion date is. If everything aligns, a contract will be drawn up. The American Institute of Architects has even put together a boilerplate construction contract (called the AIA 105) that's great for most residential projects. Sometimes the architect will be part of putting the contract together, sometimes the contractor can do it, sometimes you can do it yourself.

Ideally you have been vetting contractors while your architect has been working on getting approval from the city, so by the time that process is complete, you can have the contractor on board and ready to start.

Budget Breakdown

When it comes to the budget for your renovation, there are two main areas you can adjust as needed: the scope of the work and the cost of the fixtures and finishes. To lower the budget, we like to look for ways to achieve the end goal but limit the scope and use of expensive items. For instance, instead of completely moving a wall, maybe just opening it up a bit gives us the feeling we're looking for but at a fraction of the cost. Instead of using only expensive tile in a bathroom, maybe we use a less expensive tile on the floors and some of the walls and a more expensive tile only on one wall as a feature behind the vanity. Or maybe we get inspiration from an expensive handmade tile but find a much less expensive standard version. That's our general philosophy to keep the costs down: Use relatively inexpensive materials in most places and then upgrade in strategic areas to elevate the entire look.

When it comes to your professional team, we have some advice there as well.

- Architect: To keep the costs down, you can ask your architect to provide just the necessary filing(s) and construction drawings but not delve as much into choosing the fixtures and finishes if you feel like it's something you can tackle yourself. (We also always have the architect remove construction administration in their contract and instead handle it ourselves, only asking the architect to come in as needed.) You need to decide how comfortable you are handling this responsibility and whether you have the time and expertise needed to have the architect only come in periodically. In any case, your architect will be important in making sure the project is successful.

- Interior designer: Using an interior designer can help make your space as beautiful and cohesive as it can be, but if you find strong inspiration photos of spaces you like that you can re-create (see chapter 3), getting that designer look on your own without spending thousands on the designer, you don't need to reinvent the wheel. You can also hire a designer to do a few spaces in your home that you want to be extra special and handle the others yourself.

- General contractor: There are many things that can drive the pricing you get from a contractor. Obviously the majority of it is the cost of materials and labor, but other things come into play as well. Their availability, desire for the job, and experience level can affect the price, too—and unfortunately, unscrupulous contractors may feel like they can take advantage of you by charging higher prices. The best way to ensure you don't end up overpaying is to ask lots of questions (see page 49), get multiple quotes, and speak with several references.

Recipe for Planning Your Renovation

1. Get a reasonably comfortable initial budget (see page 34) together for your project.

2. Gather names of and referrals for professionals (architects and contractors) needed for your project from family, friends, and online and local resources.

3. Contact three to five architects (if needed) and set up meetings with each to view your space.

4. Choose an architect and begin the design phase with them.

5. Decide if you will do the design yourself, hire an interior designer, or utilize your architect's services.

6. Once a design is developed, send the plans to between three and five general contractors and set up meetings with them to see the space.

7. Gather contractors' quotes and decide which contractor is the best fit based on price and their qualifications for the project.

What You'll Need

- Some idea of what you would like to do for your project

- A budget that you are comfortable spending on the project

- Names of architects in your area

- Names of contractors in your area

- Some patience in taking these important steps before the work even starts!

Develop a Design

We wanted to give this modern Brooklyn apartment a classic feel, so we added picture frame moulding on the walls. It's an easy and cost-effective way to add character.

W e are excited to jump into the details of each room in your house, but first, let's talk about the overall design. This is something you can have fun with—really! It's an opportunity for you to think about what you like so you can give your home a healthy dose of your personal style.

One of the best ways to dream is to look for inspiration from other spaces. Spend some time on Pinterest, peruse home design Instagram accounts, flip through design magazines or books, and keep your eye open to inspiration (like that amazing tile you saw in a restaurant's bathroom while you were out to dinner). Before making any decisions, you want to expose yourself to different types of materials, colors, and finishes and understand how they can be combined. If you find an image of a space that you are totally in love with, feel free to try to copy it as closely as possible. Chances are whoever's room it is did something similar. This is a great way to be sure you're going to like the results, since you can already see them.

Next, so you'll want to organize your inspiration. Pinterest does a great job of this. You can create boards for each room, save images to that board, and include notes about what you like in them. You might actually be saying to yourself right now, "Duh, I've been doing that for years." We know! We always ask our clients to send us their Pinterest boards. We know they have them! But we also always recommend cleaning them up once you are ready to embark on your renovation journey. If you've saved seventy-eight kitchen images, it might be overwhelming. Start fresh or delete the ones that you aren't into anymore.

Once you've narrowed things down a bit, you'll want to start tying your inspiration back to actual materials. A beautiful picture of a kitchen is great, but you'll want to start understanding the components that make it a design you like. It could be the layout of the kitchen, the cabinetry style and color, the combination of open shelves and closed cabinets, the countertop and backsplash materials, the lighting placement and styles, or all of the above. At this point in the process, it's okay to just save or pin your favorite inspiration images; as you continue reading and learn which materials you need for each space, you can start assembling the details.

This living room is a total sanctuary. The soft color palette is paired with comfortable fabric, curved edges, and warm lighting.

Lookbook

After our clients send over their Pinterest dream boards, we speak with them thoroughly and ask a lot of questions. Then we walk through the space with them and talk it all out in person. Once we have a thorough understanding of what they want their home to look like and how to make it best function for them, we develop a lookbook. A lookbook is a series of mood boards for each space. Each mood board is a slide (sometimes two) for each room in the house that contains a combination of images to show our clients how the space will feel, as well as images of actual items that we are suggesting for the room. It generally helps put some direction on where the design for each space is going and gives us the opportunity to walk through with them and discuss specific ideas. You don't need us to do this for you; just take a look at the example provided on the opposite page, and we promise you can put it together yourself. We also promise it will be fun!

For instance, let's look at a kitchen mood board. We can view cabinet color, countertop material, appliances, finishes, light fixtures, and other items all in one view. This gives you the ability to visualize it all working together. You may feel like your initial choice is confirmed, or you may need to find something else that could work better. All you have to do is copy or save an image from a kitchen that you love in your Pinterest account and paste it on the slide—no technical skills required. Then as you begin specifying actual items, put those images on the mood board (with labels and links to keep things organized) to see how it all looks together. You can keep adding to it until your design is complete.

This kitchen combines different tones, styles, and textures. The finished product may look effortless, but it's essential to have a strong plan to execute a multilayered space.

Spec List

A mood board can help us get a feel for how all of the different elements of a room will work together.

The spec list includes every single item that you need to buy for your renovation. You can make it for one room or for an entire house. We recommend organizing it by floor and then by room. You might also want a general section to capture things that might not be specific to just one room, like hardwood floors that run throughout.

Some of the information that we keep in a spec list is the item (and its manufacturer and model number), a link to the web page for reference, color/finish, price, and status (ordered, shipped, delivered). This is where staying organized is so important. In a big renovation you'll be ordering a lot of stuff, and if you don't keep it organized, you might find that you forgot to order something or maybe that something was never delivered. It's also really nice to have a central place on your computer or cloud where all information can be referenced for the house. You'll do that often throughout the renovation, for example, when your contractor asks for specs on something, you can quickly send them because you can reference your spec list. You can organize on many levels with color coding, formulas, and additional info, but we'll leave that up to you and your spreadsheet wizardry.

Design Styles

If you live in a perfectly preserved craftsman and you want every detail of your home's design to be in line with that, go for it! But personally, we aren't big on sticking to a specific design style throughout the house. You can certainly put in a Scandinavian-inspired kitchen, a vintage Victorian mirror in the living room, and a Zen spa–like bathroom upstairs. Why not? You only live once—have some fun! We would just suggest that the pieces all work together in the space they are in, and that each room (especially if they flow into one another, like an open kitchen and living room) speak to one another enough to make it all work. Overall, rather than having some kind of theme for our home, we prefer finding what we like, getting inspiration from things that speak to us, and creating spaces that make us happy and comfortable. That's how we work with our clients as well. So don't be afraid to mix in vintage items, styles from different eras, and items that have meaning to you. That's how you can create an interesting and beautiful space.

Your design is something that might develop over the course of your project, but you'll want to have a lot of it worked out before the work starts. Some of your choices might determine where plumbing, electrical, and other items go, so your contractor will need to know early on. You also have to consider lead times. Some tile, appliances, and lighting fixtures may take a few months to get once the order is placed. Our recommendation is to have a fully developed lookbook and spec list for your project before you start demo. That way you have all of the design details ready to go, you know all of your lead times, and you just need to execute it to complete the project. It will also help it go much smoother and will reduce the stress on you to make decisions during the renovation itself.

It's also a great idea to have design drawings done. These are elevations (or wall views rather than overhead plan views) of certain spaces that show your contractor where to put everything. The bathroom is a great example. Understanding where the wall-mounted faucet, vanity lights, and mirror go vertically on the wall is important to know during the construction phase so that everything looks as expected when it's done and you know everything will fit before you order it. (This is also why it's important to make final choices at this point, so that all the dimensions can be taken into consideration before things are ordered.) Your architect or designer can put these drawings together for you.

Now, as far as what goes into that lookbook and spec list, read on for lots of our design recommendations for each space of your home.

This bedroom is a blend of modern and vintage elements: a velvet headboard with a mod shape, simple shelves with antique items, and classic window frames with sleek black sashes.

PAGE 60:

We adore a bold powder room. Since they are small and separated from the rest of the house, don't be afraid to embrace colorful wallpaper, funky tiles, or unique fixtures.

Know Your Design Styles

Bohemian: Bohemian style revels in bold (and plentiful) layers of color, pattern, and texture. It's a free-spirited accumulation that builds up gradually to an exclamation point (or twelve) through rattan furniture, woven wall hangings, lush plants, and vintage-inspired throws and pillows.

Coastal: Coastal style evokes a light and breezy feel by way of airy fabrics for window treatments and an emphasis on nautical or beach-themed accessories.

Contemporary: Not to be confused with modern design (mentioned opposite), contemporary design often features clean, sleek lines and swaths of solid colors—predominantly muted neutrals or bold punches of brightness. Contemporary furniture tends to be low profile, with metal frames and straight legs, and emphasizes basic shapes and forms.

Craftsman: Craftsman architecture and design often include both handsome trim and built-in elements like bookshelves and cabinetry. Exposed beams, brackets, and/or rafters are also common.

French Country: Inspired by the effortless elegance of the homes of rural France, French country design often incorporates distressed woods, aged metals, and mixed patterns such as toiles, stripes, and florals. Blue and yellow is a common color combo; other colors you see often are cream, brick red, sage green, and lavender.

Industrial: Industrial design usually includes exposed building materials (like brick), raw metals, and bare Edison bulbs. Design features are bulky and rustic feeling.

Mid-century Modern: This style started in the 1950s and was popular through the 1960s, when designers and architects embraced simplicity, functionality, and natural shapes. It consists of clean lines, tapered legs, and graceful curves.

Modern: This clean, streamlined style is rooted in minimal, true-to-use materials and an absence of decoration. You'll likely see a neutral color palette, polished surfaces, strong geometric shapes, and asymmetry.

Scandinavian: Inspired by the aesthetic of Norway, Sweden, and Denmark, Scandinavian design focuses on simplicity and functionality over decoration.

Traditional: Eighteenth- and nineteenth-century neoclassical, French country, and British colonial revival furnishings come together in traditional interiors, where classic styling and symmetry reigns. A restrained traditional palette typically features mid-tone colors and paneled cabinetry. Fabric patterns and wall treatments can range from simple solids, stripes, and plaids to florals and chinoiserie.

Vintage: Vintage design incorporates salvaged and reclaimed items (or things that look reclaimed) into the architecture and design features.

Budget Breakdown

One of the places you have the most control over savings during your renovation is in your fixture and finish choices. First of all, you can cut costs by developing your own design and choosing your fixtures and finishes yourself. Hiring a designer is undoubtedly money well spent, and they often find ways to save through trade discounts and their relationships with vendors, but ultimately, it's an additional fee to pay.

Unsurprisingly, the finishes and fixtures you choose will impact your budget. Opting for more budget-friendly options will keep your costs down, but does limit your selection. Our philosophy is to use mostly less expensive choices and upgrade in some key areas to achieve a more elevated look. It's all about knowing where to spend a bit more money. As you read on and we talk about each space, we'll point out areas where we think upgrading is a good idea.

The red wallpaper in this dining area is bold and bright. It's an unexpected way to draw light into the room.

Recipe for Developing a Design

1. Give yourself the freedom to dream big!

2. Start looking for inspiration both online and everywhere you go.

3. Organize your inspiration for each space first by floor and then by room using something like Pinterest.

4. Develop a lookbook based on your inspiration for each space.

5. As you develop your lookbook, tie it all back to actual items that you keep track of in a detailed spec list.

6. Have a fully developed lookbook and spec list for your entire project before you start demo.

Some Items You'll Need

- A Pinterest account

- Presentation software like PowerPoint or Google Slides

- Spreadsheet software like Excel or Google Sheets

PART II

Renovation Room by Room

The architectural feel
of this classic-meets-
modern kitchen is
striking. Historic
details like the crown
mouldings beautifully
play off the modern
Fibonacci chandelier
by Blueprint Lighting.

04

Kitchen Love

No two kitchens
should look the same,
but they should all
have great storage,
plenty of work or
serving space, and
seating.

We're sorry but we have to say it: The kitchen is truly the heart of the home! (We know, we know . . . big eye roll!) It just has a special way to bring people together. Sharing a meal or preparing a meal with friends or loved ones is a way that we connect with others. Invite a few (or a lot of) friends over, and what happens . . . the living room is empty and everyone is crammed into the kitchen eating, drinking, and laughing. And for that it's a magical space.

So it's not a surprise then that it's the room that comes to most people's minds when they start thinking about creating their dream home. The kitchen is a space that can set the tone for your home, but it's one of the hardest spaces to get right because there are so many parts that all need to work together. Because of this, most people find it a difficult space to figure out. Where do you begin with cabinets? What about countertops: Should you get quartz or marble? How high should you mount your exhaust hood? How do you achieve that seamless integrated fridge into the cabinetry? How do you make your kitchen look like your hundreds of Pinterest pins? There are lots of questions, but we're here with the answers.

We kept the colors very neutral and muted in this room to draw attention and focus to the gorgeous fixtures and intricate details in the crown mouldings.

Kitchen Layout

Many people want an open kitchen with clear views of the living space (if they adjoin). We have taken many walls down for clients to accomplish that. But a closed or galley kitchen can also be beautiful and functional—and it helps keep the cooking mess out of the view of guests. One of the most popular layouts is a kitchen with an island and seating to create two distinct areas for living and cooking in one space.

Whatever layout you choose, you'll want to make sure that there is ample clearance for walking and working. The minimum clearance that you need to maneuver around in any space is 36 inches, but remember that's minimum, so if you want more generous spacing, go with more. So, for instance, the kitchen island should be at least 36 inches from the other side of the counter, but a few inches more will feel roomier. You may also want to try to create the popular kitchen triangle for an efficient workflow: The stove, sink, and fridge should make a triangle or at least be positioned in a way that each is easy to access.

In this restored Brooklyn carriage house, the courtyard is a transitional space between interior and exterior—now, the homeowners can cook and entertain seamlessly.

CABINETS

There are two paths to choose from when designing, buying, and installing your kitchen cabinets. You can go with custom, designed and installed by a cabinet builder, or you can use standard-size cabinet boxes from a cabinet company.

A custom cabinetmaker will make the cabinets specifically to fit your space. They will usually come out once the space is relatively finished (framed and drywalled) so they can get accurate measurements and give you ideas about what might work best. You can also give them input on where you want the pantry, drawers, doors, pullouts, spice racks, open shelves, and anything else your heart desires, and choose the finish or color that you like. Sounds great, right? The only drawback is that it can be significantly more expensive than buying premade cabinets. A standard-size custom kitchen can set you back $40,000 to $60,000, depending on the design, and upgrades, such as the materials and finishes, can take the cost even higher.

If you decide to use standard-size premade cabinets, you can still accomplish a very beautiful design that almost looks custom. The main advantage is that it's less expensive than a custom kitchen, but it takes a bit more forethought to piece it together. You have a bunch of different-sized squares and you need to fit them in your space like building blocks.

There are three main types of cabinets—base cabinets, upper cabinets, and tall cabinets—as well as a slew of special cabinets like tall storage, refrigerator cabinets, and others. Let's look at each type one at a time.

1. Base Cabinets: Base cabinets are a good starting point when laying out the kitchen. A standard depth for base cabinets is 24 inches. The height of the cabinet is 30 inches plus 4 to 5 inches for the legs and toe kick (the panel that you typically see under the cabinet), which brings the finished height of the cabinets up to about 34 to 35 inches. The countertop will bring the height up to about a standard 36 inches, but we'll talk more about countertops later. Base cabinets come in various widths (see page 72), so you have more flexibility there.

2. Upper Cabinets: Upper cabinets have a standard depth of 12 to 15 inches, so they are set back from the base cabinets. The heights can vary, but typically they are about 40 inches high (or 30 inches high in a smaller kitchen). In some kitchens with tall ceilings, you might have space for even more height. You can stack another row of cabinets (typically shorter or the same size) on top of the upper cabinets. The upper cabinets come in the same widths as the base cabinets (see page 72).

3. **Tall Cabinets:** Tall storage cabinets are usually installed from the floor up to the top of the upper cabinets so they will span the entire height of the cabinetry. They are typically used for pantry space or to install appliances like wall ovens. The depth is usually 24 inches (so they are flush with the base cabinets), although a shallower 15-inch-deep tall cabinet can also work great for pantry space. Typical height is 80 or 90 inches, although you can stack shorter cabinets on top to achieve more height there as well.

4. **Refrigerator Cabinets:** These cabinets are made specifically to be installed over the fridge. They are usually 24 inches deep and come in the same widths that most refrigerators do: 30 inches and 36 inches.

5. **Sink Cabinets:** To install your sink, you'll need a special cabinet that's cut out on top. This cabinet should be a few inches wider than the sink; be careful not to order the same size cabinet as your sink. For instance, a 30-inch sink will not fit in a 30-inch cabinet. The measurement of the cabinet is taken from the outside; since it's usually made with ¾-inch material on both sides, the measurement of the interior space will be 1½ inches smaller, or 28½ inches in this case—too small for the sink. If you are using a farm or apron-front sink (see page 87), you also want to make sure that the cabinet door fronts leave about 10 inches above them for the sink to sit. So, if base cabinets are 30 inches high (without the legs) as we discussed above, and a farm sink is usually 10 inches high, then the cabinet doors should be 20 inches high to sit under the apron-front sink.

6. **Trash Pullout:** It's very handy to have a 15- to 24-inch-wide cabinet that pulls out for trash and recycling.

Typical widths for base and upper cabinets are 36 inches, 30 inches, 24 inches, 18 inches, 15 inches, and 12 inches, but check with the company you're getting them from about what they offer.

There are definitely a lot of options for sizes, so you might be wondering what happens when there is leftover space. For instance, if your wall for cabinets is 153 inches, you can use a 36-inch, three 30-inch, and a 24-inch cabinet, but that is only 150 inches. You'll use a filler piece (a piece of panel the same color as the cabinets) to fill the 3 inches you have left over. It's best to balance the filler pieces so that they are symmetrical. Alternatively, if you have the flexibility to build the space from scratch, you can create the exact dimensions you need.

The other components of most kitchen cabinetry are the panels. Panels cover everything that needs to match the cabinetry, excluding cabinet doors or drawer fronts. The most obvious place that you might want to use them is on the side of the fridge. Paired with an integrated paneled fridge (see page 86), you can achieve that built-in-fridge look to match the cabinetry. Remember that panels are typically ¾ inch thick, so when building your kitchen, make sure there is space for each panel. They can add up. If you panel both sides of the fridge and you put panels on either side of the range, that would be 3 inches of additional space.

You'll also need to consider the sizes of your appliances. We'll talk more about appliances later, but as you are designing your layout you can think about them the same way as your cabinets. Generally, ranges and cooktops come in 24-, 30-, 36-, and 48-inch widths. Refrigerators usually come in 24-, 30-, and 36-inch widths (although there are options for larger). Dishwashers have a standard 24-inch width. Conveniently, these are similar to the width sizes of the cabinets.

So by now you might be thinking, *Okay, I know how to configure my cabinets and appliances across the wall, but what about the height?* Let's start from the bottom and work our way up. Lower cabinets are usually 30 inches tall with a 4½-inch toe kick, which brings them up to 34½ inches. Next comes the countertop. Countertop material comes in either ¾ inch or 1¼ inches. The thinner material has a more modern look, and the thicker a more traditional look. That will bring your counter height up to about 36 inches, which is the most comfortable height for most people to work.

Upper cabinets and shelves are usually mounted to be 18 to 30 inches over the counter. Eighteen inches is short, and it's what you will typically see in smaller kitchens, apartments, or rooms with low ceilings. A larger and more high-end kitchen will usually have upper cabinets mounted 20 to 24 inches from the counter. Cabinets mounted even higher, at 30 to 34 inches, are a more modern look and are often placed that high to align with the range hood for a clean line all the way across. Keep in mind that upper cabinets mounted 24 inches or higher will be harder for some people to reach.

Typical height for upper cabinets is either 30 or 40 inches. Depending on your ceiling height, you can choose what works best for you. If there is a space above your cabinets to the ceiling, you have three options. Some modern kitchens have upper cabinets mounted with nothing above them. If you don't like that look, you can build a soffit down from the ceiling to give them a more built-in look. Finally, you can use that space for more storage by adding another row of cabinets for items you may not need often (like the two juicers we have and rarely use).

Where Do You Start?

You might be thinking, *That's a lot of information. Where do I start and how do I put all of this together?* Start by measuring your space. Draw it out on a piece of paper if you need to (there are also apps and easy-to-use software, and some of the big box stores like IKEA have online tools for this). Add any windows, doors, or other features that you need to design around. Then decide on the basic layout: which wall will the fridge and range be on, will you have an island, where will the sink be, do you want tall/pantry storage, and so on. Here are a few tips and tricks:

- Try to adhere to the "kitchen triangle rule" for an efficient workflow: The stove, sink, and fridge should make a triangle or at least be positioned in a way that each is just a few short steps from the others.

- Put tall storage/pantry units at the end of the row of cabinets or in a corner as an anchor of the design.

- Put the dishwasher next to the sink.

- It's often easier to place a sink in the island rather than a stove. Remember that you'll likely want a hood for venting over the stove, and it usually makes more sense to place it against the wall rather than in the middle of the room over the island (although there are some designs we love with that configuration).

- Be sure to save room for any panels that are needed. They are usually ¾ inch thick.

- You might find it useful to build in a pullout cabinet for trash and recycling.

- Add under-cabinet (or under-shelf) lighting. This is low voltage, which means you'll likely have to find a place to hide a small transformer, such as in a cabinet or in the wall.

- You'll want a minimum of 36 inches of clearance for all walkways, though we like 40 to 42 inches for a more spacious feel. On the other hand, putting the island out past 48 inches from the range wall might start to feel awkwardly spaced out.

You may not think of dark navy as a color to brighten or enlarge, but in this Brooklyn loft's kitchen we found this deep tone gave the room a lot of depth and intrigue.

KITCHEN CABINET STYLE

One of the first places to start when designing the look of a kitchen is the cabinet style. There are slab fronts, Shaker, raised panel, or open shelving. Slab fronts are the most modern look and Shaker has a transitional feel, while the raised panel style is very traditional. Mixing in open shelving can create a warm and cozy style.

Next, you'll want to decide what type of door design you want: full overlay, partial overlay, or inset. Full overlay covers the entire cabinet frame, partial overlay covers part of the frame but leaves some room in between where the frame can be seen, and inset has the cabinet doors and drawer fronts fit flush with the frame.

CABINET COLOR

The next design decision is whether you want your cabinet fronts to be a wood tone or painted. Wood-tone cabinet fronts can be either solid wood or veneer. Solid wood fronts are crafted completely out of a solid piece of wood; wood veneer consists of a thin layer of wood that is attached to an inner panel, usually made of particleboard or MDF (medium-density fiberboard, a low-cost engineered material that works well for cabinetry). Both are beautiful. If you want painted cabinets, a paint-grade wood or MDF can be used.

DRAWERS, DOORS, OR PULLOUTS

Designing your kitchen means you get to choose how to configure it so that it works best for you. You can have drawers, cabinet doors, and/or trash/pantry pullouts in any imaginable combination. We are fans of deep drawers for pots and pans; it's also smart to have a narrow cabinet for cutting boards, sheet pans, and serving plates so they can be stored upright on their sides. We also love a little drawer for cutlery hidden inside a larger drawer. It's nice to have a mix of sizes, as each one has a different purpose.

This kitchen may look busy at first, but notice the design "reflections" throughout—the floor and the countertops match and the lines of the tiles are reflected in the vertical wood detailing.

COUNTERS AND STONE

Now that you have your cabinets checked off, you can move on to the countertops. There are many natural stones, like marble and granite, as well as man-made options like quartz. There are also non-stone options such as wood, concrete, and stainless steel.

You can visit a stone yard to browse the options. Typically, the material is bought in slabs, and a fabricator will cut and install it. The easiest way to get your countertops is to have a fabricator come in after the cabinets are in place to measure and template. They will order the slab for you and receive it at their workshop. Then they will cut, prepare, and install.

Countertops are usually either ¾ inch or 1¼ inches thick. The smaller ¾-inch-thick counters have a more modern appeal, and 1¼ inches has a more traditional feel. Stone counters can be polished (shiny) or honed (matte). We prefer honed countertops not only for their look but also because, if you go with marble, they can require less maintenance than polished stone. Honed marble will do better disguising etching and staining. However, know that if you go with marble, you should expect some patina over time.

Extending your marble countertop up onto the wall as the backsplash is a fantastic way to draw the eye up and create continuity.

How to Get That Marble Shelf You're Eyeing in Your Inspo Pictures

It is such a beautiful sight seeing that gorgeous veiny marble shelf floating there above the kitchen countertop, but how do you achieve such a feat with a heavy piece of stone?

You definitely need to plan ahead. You will want to use a ¾-inch-thick slab of marble if you want to clad the wall for a backsplash or create a marble floating shelf. The shelf will need to be anchored into the wall. The easiest thing to do is to install metal brackets under the stone, but not many people want to see those exposed brackets, so that means we need to hide that structure that will hold the floating stone shelf in place. Depending on how deep you want your marble shelf to be, how thick you want it to be, and the scope of your project, you can choose the technique that works for you. Once you decide exactly where your shelf is going to go (we recommend 24 to 30 inches from the countertop, depending on your design), you can choose one of the following options to prepare for the installation.

OPTION 1: Mitered Shelf and Steel Brackets

Sometimes design begins in the construction phase, so planning ahead is important. The first option is to build a steel structure into the wall to support the shelf. Kitchens often have blocking in the wall (usually, thick sheets of plywood securely screwed into the studs) to support heavy upper cabinets. You'll need that for the marble shelf too. Next your contractor can install steel L brackets for the heavy marble shelf to slide onto. Drywall will go over all of it to cover up the guts. The marble shelf needs to be fabricated and mitered (cutting the edges of two pieces of stone at a 45-degree angle, then joining them to form a 90-degree angle with a continuous surface) so that a hollow space is created in the middle for the steel to slide into. If you're using ¾-inch stone and miter both edges so that there are two layers with a ½-inch slot in between, your shelf will be a total of 2 inches thick. The shelf can be up to 12 inches deep since it will have so much structural support.

OPTION 2: Embedded in the Wall

An alternative to building in so much steel structural support is to sandwich the marble in between something to hold it in place. This option requires you to use stone as your backsplash material so that it can be used as part of the support. Determining how much leverage you can get will establish how deep your shelf can be. It also requires some forethought to build a structure into the wall during construction. If you want an 8-inch-deep shelf, you'll need the shelf to be embedded about 2 inches into the wall, so the total marble shelf should be 10 inches. You'll start by putting in plywood blocking as in the first option. If your wall has metal studs, you'll also want to have some solid wood 2 × 4s to anchor onto. On top of the plywood, you'll want at least one level of drywall. When the shelf is installed, the installer will channel through the drywall, plywood, and 2 × 4s to slot in the shelf so that 2 inches of the 10-inch shelf is embedded in the wall and 8 inches is outside of the wall.

OPTION 3: Sandwiched between Two Pieces of Backsplash Stone

The last option requires the least amount of forethought, but it gets you the shallowest shelf. It also requires a stone backsplash, but the stone will need to be below and above the shelf so that it's sandwiched between the two pieces of marble, locking the shelf into place. The layer of drywall can also be slotted so the shelf can slide farther back as well. Since the shelf doesn't have as much leverage, the maximum shelf depth is about 6 inches.

Advantages and Disadvantages of Different Types of Countertop Material

MARBLE

- Pros: In our opinion, marble is the most beautiful countertop material. The richness, depth, and drama in the veining can turn any head. It's also great for cooking and baking, and it can add value to your home, as it lasts a very long time.

- Cons: Marble is a porous material and can absorb spills. This means that as long as your marble is sealed and spills are wiped up quickly, your marble likely won't stain. What it will do is etch. Staining and etching are different. Etching is physical damage to the stone caused by contact with certain substances, especially those containing acids, such as juice, coffee, citrus, wine, and tomatoes. Etching is not a stain; it is a corrosive reaction that strips away the surface layer and reveals raw marble, resulting in a dull, lighter area where the substance came into contact with the stone.

GRANITE

- Pros: A natural stone that comes in a wide range of patterns and designs, granite is a very hard substance, so it is both heat and scratch resistant. If it's properly sealed, it's less likely to stain or etch than marble.

- Cons: Granite is porous, so if not properly sealed, it can absorb liquids and stain. Although there are some very gorgeous granite options, to us they aren't quite as beautiful as our favorite marble choices.

QUARTZ

- Pros: Because it is a manufactured stone, quartz is nonporous. This means it is low maintenance and easy to clean. It's durable and stain and heat resistant. There are many variations in design.

- Cons: Although it's durable and can look very nice, the veining does look artificial and doesn't replicate the beauty of natural stone.

QUARTZITE

- Pros: A natural stone, quartzite has unique natural patterns. It's very durable, easy to clean, and resistant to heat.

- Cons: It's naturally porous and can be susceptible to stains if not sealed. It is among the most expensive of the options here. It's also more limited in color options, as it only ranges from light gray to white.

BUTCHER BLOCK

- Pros: It can have a very beautiful warm, rich tone that goes well with many designs. It's easier to cut and install than stone surfaces, and it's a more cost-effective option.

- Cons: It's very porous and requires proper sealing to prevent water damage, wear, and bacteria. And because it is a soft surface, it is more easily damaged with dents and scratches.

PORCELAIN

- Pros: Porcelain is strong and durable, made of dense and durable clay. It's resistant to stains, nonporous, and hygienic. Fabricators can add effects with pigmented glazes that bring unique colors and patterns to a porcelain slab; they do a great job replicating the look of natural marble. It's also heat and scratch resistant.

- Cons: Porcelain is usually made in thinner slabs ranging from ¼ to ½ inch thick, and the design is not integrated through the slab but is just on the surface. That means that to achieve a standard-looking countertop, the material needs to be mitered (cut on 45-degree angles and joined so that it appears ¾ to 1¼ inches thick). It can also be mitered to appear thicker than a standard countertop. It's difficult to fabricate without chipping it, which tends to push the price up.

CONCRETE

- Pros: Concrete is extremely hard and tough—it will not scratch—and very heat resistant. You can achieve a smooth, seamless surface and use varying pigments or stains to achieve the color concrete you want.

- Cons: It's a porous material, so it can stain and needs to be resealed every one to three years. Hairline cracks occur in nearly all concrete countertops, and it tends to be pricey to purchase and install properly.

BACKSPLASH

Your backsplash is going to be anywhere from 20 inches high to all the way up to the ceiling. No matter the height, it is going to be one of the things that defines your kitchen the most. Other than the cabinet fronts, it might be what catches your eye first. You can make it subtle to fade away into the design or bold to lead it. It also serves the important function of being a surface that takes splatters and splashes but they can be cleaned off relatively easily. Let's dive into some options.

TILE BACKSPLASH

The most popular material to use for your backsplash is tile. Since tile comes in so many shapes, sizes, colors, and textures, it gives you a great opportunity to build in a lot of character. The options are virtually endless. We recommend finding some inspiration for a look you love and use that as a jumping-off point. You might prefer a simple and classically clean white subway tile, or you might be drawn to a bold pop of color. Maybe you like a pattern like a herringbone or chevron.

STONE BACKSPLASH

You can wrap the same stone up your backsplash that you used on your counters for a clean and sophisticated look. If it's a marble with bold veining, it can really make quite the statement. Usually, the stone that clads the wall is ¾ inch thick, even if you are using 1¼-inch-thick stone for the counters; otherwise, it will be too thick. You'll also want to make sure the wall is very straight and plumb.

    We love the look of wrapping a natural stone from the counters up the backsplash and then capping it off with a shelf made of the same material. It's a tricky look to achieve because a lot of planning needs to be done as the kitchen is built to support the weight of the stone. It starts with some sturdy wood blocking behind the wall. Then you'll need some steel brackets screwed tightly to the blocking to mount the stone shelf on. Finally, your stone fabricator will have to build up the shelf (you'll want to use ¾-inch-thick stone for the shelf so it doesn't end up being too thick) so that there is a hollow middle to slide onto the steel brackets.

OTHER OPTIONS

Although it doesn't provide as much protection as tile or stone, wallpaper can bring a lot of character to a room when used as a backsplash. You can also use a plaster application like tadelakt (a Moroccan waterproof plaster) for a very sleek and serene look.

PRECEDING SPREAD: The light and dark wood, cool concrete counters, a custom wood-slatted and curved island, and a bold green in the backsplash of this kitchen are all visually satisfying.

APPLIANCES

Appliances can contribute to the aesthetic of your kitchen as much as its functionality. There are many sizes, finishes, and styles to choose from. Let's walk through it!

COOKING

Your options for cooking appliances are a range (burners and oven combined) or a separate cooktop and oven (which can be in a different location).

A range is easier to plan for since you just need to leave a gap in your cabinetry the size of the range. Most models are made to sit flush with the front of the cabinets (about 25 inches deep), but some professional models are deeper (about 29 inches deep) and made to sit proud of (stick out farther from) the cabinetry. So be sure to check the specs to verify you are getting the look you want. One other difference is that ovens that are included in ranges typically have fewer features than wall ovens.

A separate cooktop and wall oven require more planning since you will need to build the cabinetry around them. Companies that sell off-the-shelf cabinetry typically make special cabinets specifically for these appliances. The cooktop offers a more seamless look since the countertop can be continuous.

Gas vs. Electric?

Let's talk about gas versus electric cooking. The options are a full gas range (gas burners and oven); dual fuel range (gas burners with an electric oven); and a cooktop that's either electric, gas, or induction. Induction cooking is becoming more popular; it's a type of electric cooking but, rather than thermal conduction (an electric element transferring heat from a burner to a pot or pan), it uses magnetic induction to heat the pot or pan. Because induction doesn't use an outside heat source, only the element in use will warm due to the heat transferred from the pan, and it's cool to the touch immediately after the pan is removed. Induction cooking is more efficient than traditional electric and gas cooking because little heat energy is lost.

Your kitchen currently has either a gas line or an electric connection (usually 220 V, which is higher than a standard 110 V outlet). If you decide to switch from one to the other, you'll likely need to run the proper utility. This may seem like a no-brainer, but let's talk through it. If you already have electricity, all you'll do is unplug your existing range and exchange it for a new, similar size range. If you already have gas, the same applies. However, if you want to switch from one to another, you'll need to either run a gas line or upgrade your electrical to 220 V. Either can be a big expense—and a major construction project. There are also ranges that are dual fuel, which means they require both. Of course, the least expensive option is leaving whatever connection you already have and installing compatible appliances.

HOOD

The venting hood can be as much about the design of your kitchen as it is about the functionality. There are several hood styles and designs. The most popular is the chimney hood, but we prefer a hood insert that fits into a cabinet or a custom hood so it's more concealed. There are two ways to vent, externally or recirculating. If you're venting externally, you'll also need to run at least a 6-inch duct (check the hood specs) to an exterior wall or roof. Recirculating just filters the air through a charcoal filter and back into the room so it doesn't require a duct.

Note: You'll want to understand what size your hood is and the type you want before you purchase your cabinetry. If you're using a chimney-style hood, then you should not plan to have cabinets above your stove. Alternatively, if you plan on putting a hood insert into a cabinet, you'll need to include it in your cabinet order.

REFRIGERATOR

There are three basic types of fridges. You'll want to be sure which one fits in with your design before you order.

1. Counter-Depth Fridge: A counter-depth fridge is designed to slide into an opening and create a more streamlined appearance alongside the cabinets. Note that it will still stick out a few inches.

2. Integrated/Panel-Ready Fridge: An integrated fridge is designed to fit snuggly into the cabinetry so that it is flush with the cabinet doors. It can also be paneled to blend in like part of the cabinetry.

3. Full-Size Fridge: A full-size fridge will stick out from your cabinetry by several inches. It's not the best look for a streamlined, remodeled kitchen, but does provide the most cubic feet of storage.

SINK AND FAUCET

One of the hardest-working tools in your kitchen is the sink. There are two main options for you that contribute as much to functionality as aesthetics.

APRON-FRONT SINK

An apron-front sink has an old-world feel and adds a lot of character to a kitchen. Some of them are even centerpieces of a kitchen. They are also very functional because of their depth. Keep in mind that you'll need a special sink cabinet with lower front doors because, typically, an apron-front sink will sit proud of the front of the cabinetry about 1 to 3 inches. So, if you have cabinet doors under the sink, they will be shorter than the full cabinet height. The typical depth of an apron-front sink is 10 inches. Since full base cabinet doors are usually 30 inches tall, that means the doors under the sink will be 20 inches tall. Note that an apron-front sink can be undermounted as well, so that the countertop overlaps it, making cleanup easy.

UNDERMOUNT SINK

An undermount sink is more about functionality than aesthetics; in fact it is meant to disappear into the kitchen. They fit in more modern kitchens. Usually they are made of stainless steel and are durable and useful for sweeping anything on the countertop directly into the sink.

HARDWARE AND FIXTURES

First of all, you may not need cabinet hardware at all. Your cabinet design might include integrated pulls, or you can use push-to-open hardware, which can create very clean lines. But using hardware can be a great way to dress up your kitchen. There are many styles of hardware to choose from. One of our tricks is to use inexpensive cabinet boxes with upgraded hardware for a more elevated look.

Wow. I'm not sure if you've noticed but you just designed your kitchen! Well, at least you have a full understanding of everything you'll need to think about in order to work out the details. As you can see, there are many components to a kitchen, and you not only need to make sure you don't miss anything but you need to keep track of all of your choices. We're so excited for you that we can hardly stand it!

Budget Breakdown

The kitchen is one of the rooms that can have the biggest impact on your budget. It's often the most expensive room in the house and, because of that, it is a place where you can create the most savings.

Since cabinets are typically the highest-cost item, the first thing we advise is to decide whether you need to change the existing cabinets or simply paint or refinish them. You can even uninstall and then reinstall them in new locations if needed. If you choose to paint your cabinets, you'll want to remove all of the doors and hardware. Once they are painted, adding new hardware, new countertops, a new backsplash, and new lighting can transform the space on a relatively small budget. If you are able to paint your cabinets, it might also mean that you aren't moving things around too much. Leaving the plumbing, electrical, and gas in relatively the same locations can really keep the overall renovation cost down.

If your cabinets are not salvageable or if you are making so many changes that they won't work, there are low-cost options out there. IKEA is well known for providing afforable and stylish kitchen cabinets. Their cabinets aren't high-end, but they get the job done and will look great for many years. We often get IKEA cabinet boxes (the guts of the cabinets without the doors) and then upgrade with fronts and panels from companies that make semi-custom options like Semihandmade, Reform, and Nieu Cabinet Doors. We also love using unpainted versions so we can choose the color.

The next most expensive item in a kitchen is often the countertops. There are some nice budget options out there, like butcher block and some quartz products. We also like to visit local stone yards to see what they have. Often they have slabs of marble and other natural stone with slight defects that they are willing to sell at a lower cost. You can have your fabricator cut around the defects, or just leave them, if the defects are subtle.

Kitchen appliances are also up there on the list. We recommend going to a local appliance showroom and seeing what sales they have coming up. Labor Day, Presidents' Day, New Year's, Memorial Day . . . they have sales around almost every holiday. You can also ask if they have previous years' models that might be discounted. Chances are you won't miss whatever new bell or whistle is on the latest fridge.

Backsplash tile, lighting, faucets, sinks, and other items that go into a kitchen don't need to be expensive. Find some inspiration in a kitchen you love and re-create the look with an inexpensive version. If you look at websites like Build .com, you can put all the criteria into a search and then sort by price. You might find similar-looking items at a fraction of the cost of the expensive inspiration.

Kitchen Renovation Recipe

1. Start by understanding the measurements of the space, including the ceiling height.

2. Spend some time thinking about what layout works best for you.

3. Incorporate the workflow triangle for your appliances, and include some seating for dining or socializing.

4. Choose the fridge, range/cooktop, oven, exhaust hood, dishwasher, and other appliances that will work best for you.

5. Lay out your cabinets starting with where the appliances and sink will be.

6. Set up all of your base cabinets and then add the uppers.

7. Add some tall storage cabinets for pantry space and consider including a trash pullout next to the sink.

8. Mix in some open shelving or glass-front cabinets to add some character.

9. Choose a cabinet style and color.

10. Add countertops and a backsplash.

11. Finish your cabinets with hardware.

12. Finally, add lighting both to optimize visibility in work areas (task lighting) and to create some drama (ambient lighting).

What You'll Need

- Cabinetry: Base cabinets, upper cabinets, tall storage, and special cabinets

- Appliances: Range or cooktop, oven, refrigerator, dishwasher, exhaust hood, and others

- Sink: Apron-front or undermount

- Faucet

- Counters: Marble, quartz, granite, or butcher block

- Backsplash: Tile or stone

- Cabinet Hardware

- Kitchen Lighting

05

Bathroom Love

The primary bathroom is a place to escape and unwind. We infused this space with a moody, luxurious feel. The egret tiles by Justina Blakeney on the floor add an element of fun.

C reating a beautiful, calming, and inspiring bathroom is one of the most important things you can do to improve your home. We start our mornings and end our evenings there, so it's the place that can both set you off for a productive day and get you ready for a rejuvenating sleep. You want to feel good about the space when you're in it, and you want your guests to feel the same way. The problem is that it's often one of the dreariest and cramped rooms in the house. If that sounds familiar, don't worry, we'll get it fixed! Bathrooms are one of our favorite spaces to design, so have fun with it. And it's one of the best places to really insert your personal style.

Simple, intentional design can help your bathroom to feel like a private spa. Here, we mirrored the curve of the bathtub with an elegant arched niche.

Layout and Scope

Let's start with the layout. This is also where you have a very important decision to make. Is your bathroom renovation a refresh or a redo?

A refresh can completely transform the space and might be a DIY project. You can change all of the tile, accessories, and decor. You can paint, add wallpaper, install a new vanity, and change the light fixtures. You can even change out the plumbing fixtures—but you can't move them.

If you want to do things like swap the toilet and tub, turn a single vanity into a double vanity, or make the tub into a shower, then you are entering the redo category. Moving plumbing around is a big undertaking, and you will definitely want to call in the professionals. If your project is part of a larger home renovation, then you might be gutting everything and changing the layout anyway. So, what should you think about? (If you're doing just a refresh, feel free to skip on down to Getting Started, page 96.)

A standard bathroom size is 5 feet by 8 feet. If that's the space you have, you can fit a tub, toilet, and single vanity. If you have less space than that, it's going to be a squeeze. (We live in New York City, so we think it's totally doable to squeeze a tub into a bathroom that is 5 feet by 7 feet, but smaller spaces will likely have room for just a shower.) If you have more space than that, congratulations—you have yourself a spacious bathroom!

If you're planning a layout change or adding a new bathroom, here are some questions you might be asking:

Why Is It Called a Powder Room?

A powder room typically contains a single vanity and a toilet and is located on the main level. It can add a lot of value to your home, especially when the number of full bathrooms is limited. A powder room is essentially the same thing as a half bath. They date back to the 1700s and originally appeared only on wealthy estates. They provided a place to powder one's wig and nose. Today it's a convenience that eliminates the need to go all the way upstairs to use the bathroom . . . and it's a fun place to make bold design choices.

Should I get rid of my tub?

We rarely if ever take a bath. Until we recently had the opportunity to design and build our primary bathroom, we both have always had bathrooms with tubs. So our entire lives we have been stepping in and out of a tub to take a shower for no reason. When we designed our space, we immediately knew we wanted a huge double walk-in shower, and we love it. We do have a guest bathroom with a beautiful clawfoot tub right down the hall. So, on the off chance we're in the mood for a bath or if we ever decide to sell, we know we are covered. There is definitely a lot to think about here. We wouldn't recommend losing the tub if you don't have another bathroom with one. There are lots of people out there who won't buy a house without a tub in the primary bathroom, so, particularly if resale is very important to you, you might want to try to fit one in.

Do I have space for a double vanity?

We often see people trying to squeeze in a double vanity at all costs—even if it means no counter space, no storage, and a tight squeeze on the toilet. Having a double vanity is nice, but usually extra storage and counter space solves more problems than an extra sink. (We'll talk more about typical sizes of double vanities in a bit.)

What about that "wet room" concept I've been seeing?

If you want a walk-in shower and a separate tub but you're having trouble squeezing it all in, the wet room concept might help. Rather than creating two separate areas for the tub and shower, you create one large waterproofed area with drainage for both. It can be a bit more expensive because of the extra waterproofing and tiling you might not otherwise do, but it can be worth it to more comfortably squeeze in everything you want, while also creating a beautiful space (and likely the subject of many of your inspo pictures).

Is it okay to have a window in my shower?

Sure. Having natural light in a bathroom can be appealing, and if the window falls in the shower or tub area, that's okay. You'll just want to make sure it's made of waterproof material (not wood), and you might want to think about some kind of privacy film or frosting on part or all of the glass.

Before you lay out your bathroom, you should also consider the local building codes. There are ADA (Americans with Disabilities Act) requirements and other guidelines you might need to follow. If you have an architect on board, they can help with that.

GETTING STARTED

The tub and/or shower is typically the biggest thing in the room, so you might want to start there. In a standard 5-by-8 bathroom, it often makes sense to have the tub at the far end of the room from where you enter, with the toilet and vanity in a line along one wall. We are fans of seeing the vanity in front of you as you walk in. It's often the place where there is a lot of opportunity to create a wow factor (more on that to come!), but depending on the shape and size of your bathroom, it certainly doesn't have to be that way. Most tubs start at a standard 30 inches by 60 inches but can go up to 32 by 72. We don't like to go any narrower than 33 inches for a shower, and 36 is ideal.

This is where the wet-room concept mentioned above can come in handy. A lot of the space you need in the shower is for your shoulders and elbows. Down by your feet, you don't need as much space. So let's start with a standard 30 by 60-inch tub at the back of the bathroom, then let's put a 30-inch-wide shower area immediately next to it, with nothing separating them (so that it's one large "wet area"). The shower space is still comfortable at only 30 inches, since the space over the tub gives you the needed shoulder and elbow room. It also doesn't require the extra square footage for maneuvering and walking space between them because they are smack up next to one another. So, for instance, if you have a 5 by 10-foot bathroom, a 5 by 5-foot area toward the back can be the wet room with a separate tub and shower, and the 5 by 5-foot area in front leaves plenty of space for a 30-inch vanity and a toilet. Without putting the tub and shower in the same area, it would likely not be possible to get it all into this space.

In this garden-level bathroom, we created a large wet area (see page 95) for the tub and shower. This design makes efficient use of the space while still looking sleek and tidy.

Design

Now that you have given the layout of your bathroom some thought, we can focus on the details. You probably still have lots of questions before you can finalize your layout, so we will cover all of them as we go!

VANITY

Even though we started with the tub when we were thinking about layout, we are going to start with the vanity when we think about design. It gives you a lot of opportunity to introduce some personality into your bathroom.

The first thing to think about is what size vanity you'll need. Single vanities come in sizes between 18 and 48 inches. Double vanities typically start at 60 inches, but 72 is a popular double vanity size. It is possible to find a double vanity that's as small as 48 inches; however, having two sinks would have to be top priority for you because there will be very little counter space.

The last piece of the puzzle you need before you can finalize the size of the vanity is how much space you need for the toilet. The minimum we recommend is 30 inches with the toilet centered. More generous would be 32 to 36 inches. Over 36 inches might feel a bit too spaced out, so you might want to consider sizing up the vanity or other features in the room to use the space instead.

Now that you have the size of your vanity figured out, we can talk about the design. There are lots of options:

FOLLOWING PAGE:
For this Jack and Jill bathroom, we upcycled a dresser with drawers and cabinet space. The bold blue color is offset with simple hardware that will grow with the kids.

How to Make Your Own Vanity
Out of a Piece of Furniture

Building your own vanity out of a piece of furniture is a great idea. Not only will you save a bundle, but you will have a one-of-a-kind piece! It might be a piece of furniture you already have, or it might be something you can find inexpensively at a salvage or vintage store.

Find the right piece of furniture: The first thing you'll want to do is find the right piece. We recommend something that has cabinet doors rather than drawers because you'll need free space under the sink for plumbing. You can still use a piece with drawers, but the drawers would need to be altered or possibly even removed (you can cut a U-shape out of one or both drawers, remove them, and just attach the face as a false drawer), and remember that you'll still need access inside for the plumbing. You also want to make sure the piece is the correct width to fit the space as well as the right height. The average height for the top of the bathroom sink is between 32 and 36 inches; we like it around 34 inches. Many credenzas, buffets, and dressers are about 30 inches high, which is the perfect height to install a vessel sink. Most sinks are 4 to 5 inches high, so that will come up to the average sink height of 34 inches. If your furniture piece is 36 inches tall, you'll want to install an undermount sink, but more on that in a bit.

Installing the Sink: You have some options on how you want to install the sink. Most of the time when a piece of furniture is turned into a vanity, a vessel sink is installed, since most pieces of furniture used to make vanities are 30 inches tall. All you need to do is drill a hole, usually between 1¼ and 1½ inches in diameter. The size of the sink determines where it should be placed. Typically, we center it on the vanity top, but you can adjust it in any direction as needed, especially if you plan on using a deck-mounted faucet (a faucet that's mounted on the countertop). The sink is attached to the top of the furniture piece with epoxy, and the plumbing is installed inside the cabinet through the hole that was drilled. It will be necessary to cut out the back of the furniture piece as well so that the plumbing can continue into the wall.

Installing the Faucet: As with any vanity, you can install a wall-mounted or a deck-mounted faucet. We think that wall-mounted faucets usually work best on this type of vanity, because it means you need to drill fewer holes in your piece of furniture, and you can avoid problems with any internal parts or structure as its builder probably wasn't planning to install a faucet there. If you are going to install a wall-mounted faucet, pay close attention to how high you install it (so that the tip of the spout is 4 to 5 inches above the top of the sink) and that the spout reach (the distance from the wall to the tip of the faucet) hits pretty close to the center of the sink.

Countertop Considerations: Your piece of furniture may have a beautiful wood top. If so, you can absolutely leave it as your vanity top; that will give you the look that it is a converted piece of furniture. But you'll also want to be careful, as wood is not the best surface for a wet area. If it's a vanity that will get a lot of use, you might want to install a stone countertop or at least put on a heavy-duty finish or sealer.

Refinish or Paint: Converting a piece of furniture into a vanity might include either refinishing or painting it. If you're going to hit the salvage stores to find something, just remember when you are browsing unloved pieces of furniture that you can totally transform them with some finish or paint. See page 137 for tips on refinishing or painting furniture.

Voilà!

SINK, COUNTERTOP, AND FAUCET

Once you choose the style of your vanity, the next thing to think about is the sink type. If you chose a pedestal sink or wall-mounted sink, then you're off the hook here, since you won't need a separate sink. Or you may have also chosen a vanity with an integrated sink. If you need a separate sink, they come in two basic types: undermount and vessel sinks.

With an undermount sink, the sink sits below the countertop. This is convenient for brushing any water that splashes on the countertop right back into the sink.

A vessel sink will sit on top of the counter. Many people love the look of it, but it can make cleanup a bit more difficult.

The countertop can be any material that you would like, from a natural stone like marble to a man-made product like quartz or acrylic. It can even be wood if you're doing a vessel sink and think that you can keep the majority of water in the sink. You can stick to a simple white or a classic Carrara marble—or go for something dramatic like an Arabescato marble! This is a great place to add some personal style into your bathroom.

Another important feature of your vanity area is the faucet itself. The faucet can be deck mounted (on the countertop) or wall mounted. For a deck-mounted faucet, pay attention to how many holes need to be drilled into the countertop. Some vanities are sold predrilled, so you'll want to make sure you have a faucet that matches up to the existing holes. The most common are one hole and three holes. For wall-mounted faucets, you'll want to remember that there is a valve that needs to go into the wall. Sometimes it's sold separately from the faucet. You'll also want to make sure that you consider exactly where that valve is placed so it lines up perfectly with your sink. Finally, pay attention to the spout reach. You can find that information in the specifications of the faucet. You will want the spout reach to fall somewhere near the center and roughly 4 to 5 inches above the top of the sink.

A wall-mounted faucet can be luxurious choice to make your bathroom unique. These arched medicine cabinets from West Elm contrast the linear sconces and tile layout.

TOILET

We'll keep this pretty simple. There are two main categories of toilets: floor mounted and wall mounted. Floor-mounted toilets are more common and an easier DIY project to change. Wall-mounted toilets take up much less space and have a modern look, but since many of the mechanics are in the wall, it makes it more difficult to install or change. Since they are usually more expensive and a bit harder to maintain (if anything goes seriously wrong, it involves opening up the wall!), we use floor-mounted toilets where possible.

RIGHT:

In this pink W.C., the wall-mounted toilet saves space. It's front and center without being overstated.

LEFT:

The sleek, floor mounted toilet in this teal bathroom is a quiet complement to the bold and bright space. It's tucked away to keep focus on the beautiful floor and shower tiles.

TUB AND SHOWER

Hopefully you have already decided if you're doing a tub/shower combo, a freestanding tub, a walk-in shower, or some combination. Let's start with talking about the different types of tubs available:

Alcove Tub: An alcove tub is the most basic and most common. It's built-in and designed to have tiled walls on three sides. Typically this type has an apron front, which means the face side of the tub that is exposed to the room is the same material as the tub itself.

Drop-In Tub: A drop-in tub is similar to an alcove tub, but it's not required to have walls on three sides, and it usually doesn't include the apron front. Rather, you will usually tile the sides of the tub that are exposed to the room.

Freestanding Tub: A freestanding tub is not built in and just sits on the floor with all sides exposed. The tub filler can either be wall mounted (if the tub sits close to a wall), floor mounted, or deck mounted (mounts to the tub itself, but the plumbing still comes from the floor).

Clawfoot Tub: A clawfoot tub is a freestanding tub with vintage-style claw feet. The tub faucet can be wall mounted, freestanding, or (most commonly) mounted to the tub.

Now let's move on to the shower. As we mentioned, we prefer a shower that is at least 33 inches wide, though 36 inches or more is ideal. You can get a prefab shower pan (the waterproof insert on the floor of the shower), but we like to make a custom shower pan by waterproofing the area and installing tile. Typically, the tile will go all the way up the ceiling in the shower area, but it can stop short of the ceiling as long as it extends past the showerhead, or at least about 6 feet high. Most showers have a curb that separates them from the rest of the bathroom. This is the easiest and most common installation, but a lot of people ask us about building a curbless shower, where the bathroom floor extends just into the shower, which is separated from the rest of the bathroom with a pane of glass. It's a bit harder to build and functionally doesn't work as well, since water tends to find its way out at times, so typically the waterproofing is extended even beyond the shower. You'll want to make sure there is proper grading to allow the water to drain. It usually involves building the rest of the bathroom a bit higher so that the shower area can be graded lower.

There are two basic types of showerheads: wall sprayers and rain showers. A wall sprayer is typically mounted at an angle from the wall and can sometimes have higher pressure with various spray patterns. Rain showers are usually mounted from the ceiling or from the wall on an arm. The water pressure from them is typically less to simulate a rain effect.

To keep this vintage-inspired bathroom looking bright and open, we opted for a translucent shower curtain and a hoop shower rod matching the finish on the other bathroom fixtures.

FOLLOWING SPREAD:

We live in the bathroom as much as any other space. Adding details like a washable rug, a stool for your bath accessories, and a vase gives the bathroom character and charm.

We're inspired by the gorgeous tile-work we see throughout NYC and Brooklyn, so we love adding unique or handmade tiles to our spaces. This hexagonal tile has a subtle ombré that creates texture.

TILE

The tile in your bathroom is the best opportunity you have to introduce a design element. It's almost always the biggest feature of the room, and it sets whatever tone you desire. It can be bright and fun, calm and classic, or luxurious and high-end. We recommend finding some inspiration images you love as a jumping-off point.

First of all, you want to make sure that your tile choice works well in a bathroom. Check with the manufacturer to ensure it's wet rated and will not be too slippery when wet. Also, look to see if your tile choice is suitable for wall and/or floor applications. Not all are.

There is truly an endless amount of tile options out there. So after you have a few inspo images, ask yourself a few questions:

Do you like larger-format or smaller-format tile?

What shapes do you like (subway, rectangular, square, hex, etc.)?

Are you into marble and stone or colorful tile?

Do you like glossy or matte sheen tile?

Do you want a spa-like calming bathroom or a dramatic statement?

Now that you've chosen your tile and you're ready to order it, you need to think about how much to order. If the lead time is long, you want to make sure you get this right! Running out of tile and needing to order more can be a disaster for your timeline (trust us, we know!). Start by figuring out the square footage of the area you're tiling. Just multiply the measurements of the area. Then add 10 to 15 percent for overage. That will give you the square footage of tile you need. If it is sold in boxes, you can divide that by the amount of square foot of tile each box has (it is listed on the tile order or can be provided by the vendor). You may need to go up a bit to purchase a whole box, or down if you're comfortable with the amount of overage you'll have. If your tile is in stock and easy to get, you might be able to manage with less overage. If it is a tile with a long lead time, however, we recommend getting at least 15 percent additional. Even though you will spend a bit more on tile you might not end up using, it's better than running out! Keep in mind that some installations, like laying tile in a herringbone pattern, require more cuts and more waste, so you will need extra for that.

WALLPAPER AND PAINT

Another way you can make a statement in the bathroom is with wallpaper and paint colors. Don't be afraid to go bold. Since bathrooms (especially powder rooms) are typically smaller rooms and closed off from the rest of the house, they can be fun spaces to take some liberty with a dramatic one-off style. Remember, too, that wallpaper and paint colors can be changed relatively easily if you get tired of it or if styles move on. Here are some of our favorite designs using wallpaper and paint to make a statement in a bathroom.

PRECEDING SPREAD: Each of these bathrooms shows how combining two different colors or even two different types of tile can enhance the design-intrigue of your space.

Our Favorite Bathroom Design Tips:

Side Sconces: Putting sconces on each side of your mirror rather than above can be a more high-end look.

Floor-to-Wall Tiling: Running tile on the floor and up one wall is a nice design detail and draws the eye up to elongate the room.

Wall Mount the Toilet: Using a wall-mounted toilet can save a lot of space. We almost always put them in powder rooms since they are so small, but they can work in any other bathroom as well. Remember they do require some plumbing changes if you are switching from a floor-mounted toilet.

Skylights: Bathrooms often have no natural light. If you want your bathroom to truly be the calming and rejuvenating space of your dreams, try to introduce some. A skylight is a great way to do that even if the bathroom is in the center of the house.

Separate Toilet Room: Creating a separate toilet room in a primary bathroom can make your space feel more luxurious and more functional since it gives two people the chance to be in the bathroom at once.

Drains: Don't forget to get a drain that matches the finish of your faucet.

Exposed Plumbing: If you are using a wall-mounted sink with exposed plumbing, you might want a nice-looking P trap that matches the finish of your sink. (A P trap is a U- or P-shaped bend in a drain or waste pipe that traps a pocket of water, which blocks foul-smelling sewer gases from traveling through the pipe into your home.)

Wow, congrats! You designed a bathroom and we know it's beautiful!

If you still associate wallpaper with your grandparents' home, think again! Modern wallpaper can be elegant, playful, whimsical, or funky.

Budget Breakdown

There's lots of savings to be had in a bathroom renovation both in the construction and in the fixtures and finishes.

First of all, if it's possible to keep all of the plumbing in the same locations, you can save a lot on the construction costs. You can even take things a step further and try to save some or all of the items in the bathroom. You might find that changing the vanity, mirror, lighting, and paint or wallpaper is just the refresh your bathroom needs.

If you're done with the current bathroom and you are ready to blow it up, we don't blame you! But there are still ways you can save. There are a few things that you can adjust in your design to keep the budget low:

- A custom walk-in shower is the most expensive option. Installing a tub or using a prefab shower pan can reduce waterproofing costs. Consider whether the upgrade is worth the cost to you.

- Installing a claw-foot tub can eliminate the need to do much expensive waterproofing at all. And you might be able to find one from a salvage store at a great price.

- If you do use a vintage claw-foot cast-iron tub or you have an existing cast-iron tub, it can be reglazed (interior) and painted (exterior) so that it is just like new again.

- Installing a wall-mounted toilet is more expensive than installing a floor-mounted model. Not to mention the wall-mounted versions will cost more to buy.

- Limit how many surfaces are tiled. Only tile to the ceiling in the shower or bathtub area and either up to only half height on the other walls or not at all.

- Don't use a large format tile. Some contractors charge more to install a tile that's bigger than 24 inches because it's more difficult to install and takes special equipment to cut.

- There are a lot of very expensive options for tile and plumbing fixtures out there. And while they are nice, there are no doubt super budget-saving versions that could give you a very similar look. Get inspiration from the expensive versions and then look for alternatives that are close but a fraction of the cost.

- The vanity can be one of the most expensive things in the bathroom. Get creative and build one yourself out of a piece of furniture (see page 100). Not only will you save potentially thousands of dollars, but you'll have a one-of-a-kind piece!

- Plan to use prefab shower glass rather than a custom one. Or just use a shower curtain.

- A lot of people love the look of a curbless shower (see page 106). They are gorgeous, but there are drawbacks, including the price. Waterproofing is more expensive because it will be custom, and heavy-duty waterproofing also needs to extend a few feet outside the shower since there is no curb to potentially stop water. Finally, in order to accommodate a pitch for drainage, the entire bathroom floor has to be raised a couple of inches. Go with a shower with a curb to save some of that extra expense.

Bathroom Renovation Recipe

1. Start by determining if your renovation is a refresh or a redo.

2. Decide what layout is best for you; whether you want a tub, shower, or both; and what size vanity you would like.

3. After you choose the size of your vanity, choose some of the design elements for the room.

4. Understand what type of sink, countertop, and faucet will work best for you.

5. Get your toilet chosen and set in place.

6. Configure your tub and shower.

7. Choose your tile. Have some fun or make your bathroom the spa-like, calming space of your dreams.

8. Finish the space off with lighting, wallpaper, and paint.

What You'll Need

- A solid layout
- Vanity
- Sink(s)
- Faucet(s)
- Toilet
- Tub (if your bathroom will have one)
- Tub filler (a special faucet designed to fill a bathtub)
- Shower
- Shower faucet
- Drain for all plumbing fixtures

06

Living Room Love

This living room is completely tranquil and modern. We put back a marble fireplace where one had been removed and restored the stained glass for vintage character.

I f the kitchen is the heart of the home, is the living room the . . . face? No other room inside the home is meant to be as public as the living room. Yes, we design our living rooms to be cozy places for the family to gather, but they are also meant to be a space for guests, so the room should feel comfortable to them, too. They are one of the primary places in the home where we can express ourselves, our style, and our lives to the greatest degree. They are the room where we tell a story of who we are through our color and furniture choices, and through the items we display: objects we've collected while traveling, photos, art. They give us the opportunity to create a mood and a vibe apparent to anyone who enters the home.

A neutral palette is a nice backdrop for layering a room. Add unique shapes, textures, and patterns, to create lots of visual interest in the space without a lot of color.

You might think that from a renovation and construction perspective, there isn't much going on in the living room. That is true compared to the kitchen and bathrooms, but there are definitely things to think about when laying out and designing this space.

Depending on the scale of your renovation, you might be reconfiguring the layout of your home. Will you open up the kitchen to the living room to create an open plan? Will it include a dining area as well? Or do you want a cozy separate space for dining?

A medium-sized living area is about 12 by 15 feet. (This is not necessarily the size of the room but the area where the furniture lives.) That gives you enough space for a couch, a coffee table, two armchairs, and a lamp. If your living room will be an open plan, then you should have some room to navigate around that area. If your living room is a separate room, you might want it to be a bit larger than that so that it doesn't feel too cramped.

One of the first things that we recommend thinking about is what *you* will primarily use the space for. Is it mainly for entertaining guests? Is it for

Don't be afraid to move the furniture off the wall. Here, we created a sitting space in the middle of the room, anchored by the fireplace.

relaxing with the family? Are you and your family TV people, and do you plan on sitting back, remote in hand, each evening? Are you board game lovers? Is it to admire a view? We could go on, but the point is to go into a renovation with a clear understanding of the room's primary use. There may be secondary uses to consider as well. For instance, we are TV people. Our idea of a relaxing evening is to sit back and watch our favorite shows. That means we need to have comfy furniture facing the TV and somewhere to put our feet up. It might sound obvious, but we needed to design our living room with a wall directly in front of the couch, opposite and not perpendicular to it, for the TV. Have you ever viewed a home or an apartment to rent or buy and you stand there wondering where in the world a TV can go? Before our renovation, the room lent itself to the TV on a wall perpendicular to the couch, so we moved some things to create a space in which we are able to thoroughly relax and feel comfortable.

The room's secondary use for us is entertaining guests. Our TV-centric layout didn't prevent this at all, because we made sure the space also facilitates conversation.

Central Feature

One of the best ways to anchor your living room is to use or create a central feature. It makes your space feel grounded and adds character to the room. An obvious example would be a fireplace. If you have one, you may inherently know it will be the focal point of the room, even if it's not working. Furniture placement will likely surround it in a way that it anchors the room. The central feature can also be a large picture window that helps you align the furniture. If the room doesn't have something that can be the central feature, you can create one. It could be built-in bookshelves, recessed arch openings with shelves, or maybe even a large piece of artwork over the couch.

FURNITURE PLACEMENT

Whether or not your living room will be a separate space, we recommend making it feel that way. So even if your living room is part of an open-plan living area, make it feel cozy and add some features that will delineate the room. Create a conversation area by placing the furniture in a way that makes it comfortable for guests to converse. Usually that means setting an armchair or two opposite or perpendicular to the couch with a coffee table between them. Use an area rug and lamps to create a cozy space and make it feel like a room within a room.

LIGHTING

Pay attention to where the lighting is placed above. A well-placed chandelier in the center of the living room and dropped a bit lower over the coffee table area can even be your room's central feature. We are fans of layering the lighting, so rather than having one bright fixture, go with something that only lights part of the area and add other light sources. If you have recessed lighting or a central light fixture, put them on dimmers so that you can lower the light and create smaller, cozy lighting areas with lamps, wall washers (which light a wall or illuminate artwork), floor lamps, and other ambient lighting sources. You can turn things on or off to create different moods in the room.

OPPOSITE:

This family space aligns with the windows in the back of the home and gets much cooler, crisper light. We wanted to reflect those cool tones in the stark white of the two hanging lamps.

BELOW:

The natural light coming in through the main windows and the vestibule area makes this space feel warm and inviting. We added a statement chandelier to keep that glow into the evening.

Architectural Detail

Anytime we design a space that has some architectural detail, it is always everyone's favorite part of the room. There are many ways to do this, so let's talk about a few:

1. Nooks: Creating a recessed area for shelves or art can really make a room feel unique. There is often space in the walls that can easily be used. If you're already renovating, it probably won't cost much more to create the nook than to build a flat wall. With all of the 90-degree angles that go into a house, we love to introduce some curves. A recessed nook with an arched top is practically a calling card of ours in every home we design.

2. Curved Corners and Walls: Speaking of curves, we dare you not to make every corner in your house 90 degrees. Cutting off the 90-degree hard corner and curving a wall can really open up a space. There isn't one time that we decided to curve a wall that we didn't then say every time we walked by it, "Wow. Can you imagine how cramped it would feel to have a hard-edged corner here?" It may not work in every home, but keep it in mind as a way to add an interesting feature and open up some space. Also remember that you can use a radius corner bead to round edges as well.

3. Arches: Arches are one of the most timeless ways to build in architectural detail. They have been used for centuries to make a space beautiful. Instead of a squared opening between rooms or a square doorway, add an interesting detail and arch it!

4. Wall Moulding: We often work in historic homes where wall or picture-frame moulding is common, but even if you live in a new condo, you can add so much character and detail by incorporating this into your design. It's also inexpensive and relatively easy to do, although it can take some time. One of the first things you'll want to do is choose the moulding design you'll use. There are many sizes and styles, from a chunkier profile to a slimmer one. We like to use something between 1¼ inches and 1½ inches. The next step is to plan the picture frame boxes, which can be the hardest part. One of the keys to making it look great is even and consistent spacing. You need to measure carefully and plan. The next step is to arrange it vertically. You can have one box, an upper and lower box, a chair rail in the middle, or even a picture rail across the top. It's your preference, as long as the spacing is consistent.

Adding twin recessed arched nooks to this dining space adds architectural detail where there was none. It also conceals the radiator in plain sight!

5. Built-Ins: Built-ins can create architectural detail and be very useful for storage. Not only do the shelves and cabinets themselves give the room character, but they also provide the opportunity to display interesting items and books that show off your personality and style. Images of white or wood-toned units might come to mind, but don't be afraid to have some fun. We like painting built-ins with bright and vibrant colors. For an extra bold look, paint the entire room and the built-in the same rich color.

6. Mouldings and Trim: Mouldings serve a vital purpose in your design. They are used to cover the gaps and hide the unattractive places where materials come together. Your baseboards cover the gap where the flooring meets the wall, as well as provide a more durable surface for the beating that area of the wall takes. It goes beyond that though; many mouldings are ornate and decorative or intentionally less so. We're going to cover mouldings and trim in more detail in chapter 9, but what you should know now is that mouldings are an important detail to complete your space, and the living area is often where the most decorative mouldings go.

7. Paint: Finally, the simplest way to create architecture detail without picking up a hammer is to pick up a paintbrush! Paint an arch as a backdrop to shelves, a desk, or other furniture; you can also paint stripes or other shapes on the wall to accomplish the same thing. Or use two tones of the same color (or two contrasting colors) to create the illusion of wainscoting on your walls.

These custom built-in shelves combine curves and straight lines to give a retro silhouette. The warm wood in the bookshelf, the door frame, and the fireplace mesh well together.

How to Install
Picture-Frame Wall Moulding

Picture-frame moulding can add charm and detail to any room. It's usually found in historic homes, but we have also put it into newly renovated homes and modern high-rise condos. It's a relatively easy project to DIY.

WHAT YOU NEED:

- Tape measure
- Painter's tape
- Moulding
- Level, laser level, and/or chalk line
- Miter saw or miter box and handsaw (available at hardware stores)
- Fine grit (180–220) sanding paper or block
- Construction adhesive
- Nail gun or hammer
- 1-inch nails
- Wood filler
- Paintable caulk and caulk gun
- Paintbrush
- Primer (optional)
- Paint

STEP 1: Measure and choose the design.

Start by measuring all of the walls where you're planning to install moulding. It's okay for the boxes of moulding to be different sizes, but you want them to have consistent spacing. There are many different designs to choose from. You can place one box vertically or split it into two. You can have a chair rail in the middle or a picture rail at the top. You can have a double moulding box or a single. You can even create extra angles at the corners for more detail.
As you're planning your design, first decide on the number of boxes and the preferred spacing between boxes. If you want your boxes to all be equal width, use the following equation to determine how wide they should be: width of wall — (space between boxes × number of boxes + 1) / number of boxes = width of each box.

STEP 2: Prepare the mouldings to be installed.

Now that your design is planned, we recommend taping it out with painter's tape to make sure everything looks like you want and the spacing is consistent. You might find that your pieces of moulding run into outlets or other features on the wall. You can now make slight adjustments to avoid that.

One of the most important things is to make sure that all of the moulding is straight on the wall. You can use a level on each piece of moulding as it's being installed or you can use a laser level or snap a chalk line.

Next, cut each moulding on a 45-degree angle using a miter saw. The miter box has grooves that guide you to cut the moulding pieces on a perfect 45-degree angle. Cut enough moulding for the first box and make sure you have the process down, then cut the remaining moulding. Use your sandpaper or sanding block to knock off any rough edges on the cuts.

STEP 3: Install the moulding.

You need to start with one side of the box; we usually start with the bottom. If you already taped out where the moulding should go and you have a laser level or chalk line on the wall, it should go on quickly. Run a bead of the construction adhesive on the back of the moulding and press it into place on the wall, making sure it's level. Once you confirm the placement, nail it into place.

Next, you can move on to the side pieces. Use adhesive to connect the 45-degree cut end of one side piece to the bottom piece, using your level to be sure it's installed straight, then nail it in place. Repeat with the other side. After both side pieces are installed, you should be able to put a level horizontally on the top edges and confirm that they are level. (If you want some flexibility, you can nail in only the lower half of the side pieces and adjust a bit when putting in the top piece.) The top piece should now fit perfectly into the two 45-degree cut edges of the side pieces.

That should complete your first square. Don't worry if there are small gaps at the 45-degree cuts and nail holes. Those will all be filled with the wood putty and caulk in the next step.

Move on to the next box and repeat until all of the mouldings are installed.

STEP 4: Use wood filler and caulk.

This is what is going to make your work look really professional, so it's a very important part of the project. It may be a little tedious and time-consuming, but you don't want to skip this step.

Once all wall moulding is installed, fill all the nail holes and gaps at the corners of each box with wood filler. Once the wood filler is dried, you can sand off any excess so that it's nice and smooth.

Now it's time to caulk all of the mouldings. Apply a thin bead of caulk between the moulding and the wall and then wipe the caulk smooth using a wet finger or paper towel. Take your time and make sure it's all smooth and clean. The caulk will cover up any gaps and help secure the mouldings to the wall.

STEP 5: Paint the moulding.

Once the caulk has dried, it's time to paint! We like to paint picture-frame moulding the same color and sheen as the wall. If your moulding didn't come primed, you'll want to start by brushing on a primer. Then you can paint the moulding with your wall paint. If your walls are already painted with the same color and sheen, you probably won't need to paint the entire wall, but if it isn't, you will need to repaint.

Sit back and enjoy your picture-frame moulding!

Design Details

Now that the basics of your living room are set, it's time to layer in the details. Think about how you want the space to feel, not just how you want it to look. Here are some of our top tips for bringing your own personal style into your living room.

1. **Choose a Starting Point:** There are a lot of components that go into living room design, so our first piece of advice is to find a starting point. This is usually one of the larger pieces in the room. For us, often it's the sofa, but sometimes it's a rug or an armchair; it could be a piece of art or even a color. Maybe you took our advice a few sections back and painted the entire room and built-ins a deep rich color; that might be your starting point because the next decision might be to make sure the larger pieces of furniture provide contrast to that deep rich color.

2. **Create Contrast:** Even if you're a fan of nothing but neutrals, one of the first things we do when designing a living space is to make sure there is some contrast. Let's continue with our example of the room we painted a deep rich color, including the built-in. Our next decision would be to bring in a light-colored sofa and rug to provide contrast to all that deep color. If your walls are white and your starting point is a light-colored sofa, you might want a darker tone on the rug or an armchair. Or maybe if you want only light tones in the larger pieces of furniture, the contrast comes from the throw pillows.

3. **Bring in Some Color:** Even if you typically don't gravitate toward bold colors, we recommend bringing in some color somewhere. If you want to avoid saturated colors on the larger and more permanent features, bring it on items you can change easily, like a throw or pillows.

4. **Make It Cozy:** No matter how open and lofty your room is or isn't, you want to make your living space feel cozy and welcoming. Create a conversation area by placing the furniture in a way that makes it comfortable for guests to sit and talk. Use an area rug to delineate this area from the rest of the space. Living rooms feel welcoming with a sofa, coffee table, and armchairs arranged facing each other so that it invites conversation. Install a lower-hanging light fixture in the center. Use floor lamps or table lamps to create some moody lighting and make the space feel homey, even when they are turned off.

Consider this room without the pouf: It's still a fantastic space with the deep green of the sofa and the rich black coffee table. But adding the pouf creates a welcome contrast.

5. **Layer in Different Textures:** It's as important to us to layer in different textures as it is to create contrast in color. Vary the materials with your rugs, pillows, throws, and even furniture. If you already have wooden side tables, why not look for a coffee table that's a different material, such as stone or metal. If your couch is upholstered, maybe the armchairs can have some wood elements. If your sofa is leather, the armchairs can be upholstered.

6. **Bring in Something Organic:** Bringing something living into a space really breathes some life into it. Find a houseplant or two that will hold up to even brownish thumbs. (Unless you have a green thumb, in which case, go wild.)

7. **Work in Some Interesting Items:** Make sure to find some interesting items to display. Our best advice is to mix in some vintage items. Visit a few local vintage shops and look for armchairs, side tables, credenzas, coffee tables, floor lamps, and art. One or two vintage items can really make a space special. And we never style a living room without adding some books: design books, travel books, architecture books, nature books—whatever you're personally interested in. It helps you tell your guests the story of who you are. Finally, add some items that are significant to you. These might be from your travels, family pictures, heirlooms, or just things that have stuck with you for a long time.

The wood inlay in this floor is stunning and intricate, while the clean lines of the vintage chair is structurally open and subtle in this corner.

How to Refinish, Paint, or Repurpose a Piece of Furniture

STEP 1: Wipe down and prep the furniture.

The first step is to wipe down, inspect, and prep the piece. It also might make sense to take it apart, as pieces are usually easier to sand and refinish that way. For example, if the top of a table comes off the base, you can separate them and remove any drawers.

STEP 2: Sand the surface.

Once the piece is thoroughly cleaned, the next step is to sand off the existing finish using an orbital sander. Have sanding discs in various grits on hand. If the finish is really difficult to get off, you can use a lower-grit sandpaper, like something in the 100s.

STEP 3: Clean off and prep the furniture for staining or painting.

Once the original finish is completely removed, wipe down the entire piece with a damp cloth. Let the piece dry, and then inspect it to see if you need to do any sanding touch-ups before you begin staining. If your furniture also has cracks or holes, you can first patch them with a filler that matches the color and grain of the wood.

STEP 4: Seal the wood.

Sealant protects wood furniture and creates a smooth base for stain or paint to stick to.

Apply a generous coat of sealant all over the furniture. Wipe away any excess with a clean cloth. Once the sealant is dry, use fine-grit sandpaper to smooth the surface. Clean off any excess wood dust.

STEP 5: Stain or paint your wood furniture.

The next step is to apply the new coat of paint or wood stain. Use a paintbrush to brush on your preferred paint or stain, and let it dry completely. Check the piece and decide if another layer is necessary. (For staining, it might be easier to use a rag, but be sure to also wear disposable gloves.) After the stain sits for about 5 minutes or so, wipe off all of the excess stain with a clean rag.

STEP 6: Apply a wood finish.

After the piece has thoroughly dried (usually overnight), the last step is to apply a coat of wood finish. (This step is less important for painted furniture because the paint itself provides a layer of protection.) Since it sat drying for several hours, wipe down your entire piece with tack cloth to remove any stray pieces of lint or dust. Use a paintbrush or a rag to apply the finish. Let it dry completely. Look at the piece of furniture and decide if a second coat is necessary. Between each finish coat, you can sand lightly by hand with very-fine-grit sandpaper (over 200 grit). This will help create a nice smooth finish, but don't sand the final coat.

Enjoy your refinished piece of furniture!

To Dine or Not to Dine?

Increasingly in the homes in which we work, the living space also includes a space for dining, as opposed to a separate dining room. An open living, dining, and kitchen plan can create an inviting entertainment space. (Separate formal dining rooms aren't as common, especially if space is tight, but if your home already has one or if you prefer the more traditional layout, they are perfect for a cozy meal.)

To make your dining area feel like a separate, well-considered, cozy space even if it's part of a much larger room, start at the top. The pendant or chandelier over your table sets the tone for the space. We like a chandelier that really makes a statement! The bottom should be roughly 30 to 36 inches above the table. (You will need to know your ceiling height when you order the chandelier.) Sometimes they come with a fixed stem, but you need to specify the length. All you need to do is measure your ceiling height, subtract the dining table height (typically 30 inches), subtract the measurement of how far you want the bottom of the fixture to be from the table (we suggest 36 inches), note the height of the fixture itself, and voilà—you have your stem length.

The table that you choose will contribute significantly to the design of your dining space. One of the first decisions to make is whether you want a square, rectangular, round, or oval table and how many chairs you want around it. A round table can encourage conversation since it gives all of your guests equal access to one another, but a rectangular table might be better for your space. Make sure you are choosing the right size table for the area. You'll want about 36 inches of clearance around the table so that the seating is comfortable, and you'll need about 24 inches for each place setting (if you have a 72-inch table, for example, you should be able to seat three people on each of the longer sides). You can also insert your personal style when choosing the design of and material for your dining table and chairs. A beautiful walnut table can be a showstopper; a mid-century modern table with tapered, streamlined legs can create a mood; and a vintage table with mismatched vintage chairs can tell a story. Whatever you choose, make sure it's something you envision your family and friends gathering around for years to come.

We've arrived at the bottom, the last big item that you might want for your dining room: an area rug. Something with a pop of color could spice up your dinner parties, but feel free to keep it neutral. The rug can also help create a separate area for your dining table if it's part of the living space, but make sure it also speaks to the rest of the room.

Finally, the dining area is the perfect place to display some interesting art pieces. A large painting or even a gallery of smaller items can give the space some visual interest. We really enjoy bringing picture-frame moulding into this space as well. This area of your home is all about spending time with friends and family, so make it a comfortable space where you'll want to linger for hours.

Budget Breakdown

Other than the general construction budget for the house (walls, floors, electrical, HVAC, etc.), there are likely two main places in your living room where the budget goes and can potentially get out of control: built-ins and furniture.

1. Built-Ins: We have a simple fix for costly custom built-ins: Just don't do them! You can always get an inexpensive bookshelf, hutch, or credenza for storage. That said, custom built-ins can be very beautiful and useful, so if you do want to include them on the cheap, create recessed areas inexpensively with drywall while you're building the walls and put in floating shelves. It's much less expensive than building the entire unit out of finished wood and will give you the look and functionality of custom built-ins without an enormous price tag.

2. Furniture: We have seen more people than we can count renovate their home beautifully and forget to save any of their budget for new furniture. We get it. You can always get that later, right? But after you spend months making every space perfect, you might not be too excited to see your tired furniture in your newly renovated home. So, what can you do to make sure your furniture is doing your new home justice without breaking the bank? When we have a seriously low furniture budget, we always start with what is already owned. Everything may not be coming into the new house, but no doubt there are a few pieces that can. We also pay attention to what can be repurposed, refreshed, and reupholstered. If it's a good piece but the wrong wood tone, that can be changed. If the upholstery is stained or worn, reupholster it. The next thing we do is look for vintage or used items. Websites like Etsy and Facebook Marketplace are a great place to find items, often in good condition or which can be easily refurbished. Finally, you can often get great deals on furniture from the big box stores. Look for inspiration from custom pieces and try to find similar items for much less at the big stores. We do recommend mixing in some unique pieces as well, so you don't end up with too much of a catalog look.

PRECEDING PAGE:

In comparison to the fresh cream walls, this walnut table from Rejuvenation becomes the immediate focal point of the room. Its warmth makes it incredibly inviting for a cozy meal.

Recipe for Renovating and Designing Your Living Space

1. Start by thinking about what you'll primarily use the space for.

2. If you are gut-renovating the house, spend some time thinking about what layout works best for you: open plan or separate rooms.

3. Remember that your living space likely serves dual purposes of providing you and your family with a place to relax and also a space in which to entertain guests.

4. The living room offers one of the best opportunities to put your personality and personal style on display. Make it fun, beautiful, and comfortable, and show your personality.

5. Anchor the room with a central feature.

6. Place your furniture in a way that encourages conversation.

7. Make it cozy by using an area rug, lamps, and interesting design items.

8. Add some architectural detail.

What You'll Need

- Furniture: Couch, armchair(s), coffee table, side table(s), area rug, lamps

- Design: Vintage items, interesting pieces, and objects that have meaning to you.

- An element of architectural detail

07

Bedroom Love

From the orientation
of the bed to the
lighting surrounding
it, your bedroom is
the most intimate
space in your home
and you should design
it as such.

Your bedroom should be a place that helps you relax and unwind. For us, the space needs to look good to feel good. We've seen plenty of people pay a lot of attention to the more public areas of the home, like the kitchen and living room, and ignore the bedroom. Don't underestimate the importance of making your most personal space the best it can be for your own enjoyment of your home. A well-designed and comfortable bedroom helps you start and end each day on the right foot!

Now, how can you make it feel like the most comfortable, beautiful, and luxurious hotel where you had the best sleep of your life? Let's get to it!

Think of your bedroom as a calming space to rest your head and your mind.

Start with the Bed

It's the biggest and most important thing in the room, so we need to start there. First, you'll need to decide what size bed to get. We recommend getting the biggest bed that will comfortably fit in the space. If you can fit a king, go with a king! We started with a full-size bed and thought moving to a queen would be a big upgrade. It was, for a while, but we realized that we should have gotten a king, and our bedroom was (just!) big enough for it. So only a couple of years after upgrading to a queen, we gave it away and had to buy a new mattress, bed frame, and headboard.

Before you finalize your decision on what size bed, you should have an idea of where the bed will go. There might be one wall in your bedroom that's the only obvious option for the bed, or there might be a couple of options. You might even have to build your bedroom so that there is a comfortable place for the bed to live. We have moved doors, bathroom entrances, and closets and even extended an awkwardly placed old fireplace bump out in our own bedroom to make sure we had a good backdrop for our bed. If your bed is shoved into a corner, up against a wall, not centered, or blocking windows, you may struggle with making the room feel comfortable and inviting. So, make sure that the room is big enough for your bed and that you plan the design around where the bed will go.

We aren't the biggest advocates for bringing feng shui concepts throughout a house, but the bedroom is the place where creating a positive and relaxing environment is very important, and many of the concepts are practical and smart. One of the essential ideas when applying feng shui to your bedroom is the placement of your bed. The concept suggests placing your bed away from the door but not beside it. Basically you want to have a clear view of anyone entering the room. The bed should be lifted off the ground and backed with a well-made headboard that feels solid and supportive while you sleep. Whether or not you subscribe to the ancient Chinese concept of qi, this is excellent and practical advice to making your bedroom more comfortable.

Once you decide the best wall for your bed, don't forget to save room for side tables and lighting on each side. Side tables give you a place to put a glass of water or a book, and they help your bedroom feel more comfortable and lived in. If you're planning for hardwired sconces, you'll want to make sure the electrical boxes fall at the center of the side tables. Knowing the size of the bed and side tables is important to figuring that out.

Orient your bed in a way that feels inviting when you enter the room, but also relaxing and comfortable when lying in it.

Primary Suite and Other Bedrooms

If you are renovating your home, building a primary suite with ample closet space and an en suite bathroom will not only help your home be more functional for you and your family but can increase its value as well. Being able to prepare for the day or wind down for sleep fully within your own personal space can bring a sense of calm and help you feel more relaxed. Imagine being able to retire to your personal suite without having to go back out to the public space when you have overnight guests. If your house doesn't have a primary suite already, consider stealing space from the main bedroom or from a neighboring bedroom to create one.

Most likely your home will have more than one bedroom, so we recommend following the same guidance in this chapter for other bedrooms as well but on a smaller scale. The rooms may have less closet space, smaller beds, and (most likely) no en suite bathroom, but the rest is very much the same.

Closet Space

Many of us struggle with keeping tidy and organized. Trust us, we do too! But all too often it's a result of our space just not working for us the best it can. Nowhere is that as important as in your bedroom. It will likely be difficult to get the restorative rest you need if your bedroom feels chaotic. What's the best way to solve that problem: closet space! If you have specific and ample space for your clothes and other items, it's much more likely they will end up there.

We'll talk all about making your closet as organized and functional as possible in the next chapter, but when designing your bedroom, make sure you devote enough space for storage. Even if it means sacrificing a little bit of space in the bedroom, it will be worth it.

Many people associate closet space with a walk-in closet. Sure, a walk-in closet can offer a lot of storage if you have the space for it, but if you don't, a well-designed reach-in closet or even millwork (using cabinetry for your closet) can be just as useful. Remember that a lot of a walk-in closet is dedicated to walking space. So you might be able to more easily fit a 2-foot-deep reach-in closet across a wall rather than trying to create an entire extra room for your clothes.

A clear, visual sight line through the closet and bathroom make this primary suite feel luxurious and open.

Make It Cozy

Making your bedroom functional is important, but it is only half the equation for a truly comfortable space. So, now that your bedroom has all of the essentials, it's time to make it inviting and cozy.

1. Colors: We love to paint a soothing color on the walls. Dark blues and greens are our favorites. You can also bring in color in the drapes and linens instead if you like. Add a couple of throw pillows in a contrasting color, and your bedroom will already feel more inviting.

2. Area Rug: Just as in your living room, placing an area rug under your bed can anchor it in the space and make the room feel cozier. Once you have crawled into bed from a comfy area rug or stepped out of bed onto one, you'll never go back! It's also a great way to bring some more color and texture into the space.

3. Headboard: A solid headboard can make your sleep more comfortable. Headboards come in all kinds of different styles and variations. There are warm wood tones, plush upholstery, leather, or something textual like cane webbing. Our advice is to look at some pictures of bedrooms that make you feel relaxed and happy. Chances are the style of the headboard has a lot to do with that. From there you can start to figure out what style will work best for you.

4. Bed Linens: Dressing your bed is all about creating layers of comfort. A bed that looks layered and plush is going to be more inviting than one with just a sheet and a pillow.

    *   Sheets: We spend a lot of time in our beds, so splurging a little bit on some really nice linens can be worth it. You'll feel more comfortable in your bedroom if you can't wait to crawl in bed and you don't want to get out of bed in the morning. Comfy sheets are the foundation. We recommend looking for something in the 300 to 400 thread count range. Percale or sateen sheets will make for a comfortable night's sleep, but go with satin for a more luxurious look and feel.

    *   Duvet: Your duvet is another thing that will make your bed more comfortable. It usually has two pieces: the duvet insert and the duvet cover. The insert is the fluffy part and can be either down or a synthetic material. You can even get a

Don't be afraid to add bold colors to the bedroom; it's not only neutrals that can give a warm, inviting feel to the space.

lightweight duvet insert for summer and a warmer insert for winter. The cover is the part you see and touch, and it can be removed and washed. You can swap it out for different looks.

- Pillows: Of course you'll want some comfy pillows for sleeping, but don't forget some pillows for styling too. Start with two double-stacked sleeping pillows for a hotel-quality, comfortable feel. Then add two or three throw pillows in contrasting colors and different sizes to layer it up.

- Throw or Bedspread: We tend to style a bed with an attractive duvet cover and a statement throw draped across the foot of the bed, but you can also go with a bedspread for a more formal look. Having the throw at the foot of the bed provides the final layer that makes your bed look as comfy as can be, but it also gives you a little extra warmth if needed while you're sleeping.

Lighting

Lighting is very important to making your bedroom feel cozy. You will likely have a main light fixture in the center of the room. We really like using a modern chandelier or pendant that hangs down from the ceiling a bit. Bringing the main light fixture closer to the bed, rather than way up on the ceiling, gives the room a cozier feel.

Then you'll want a bedside lamp on or a sconce over the bedside tables on each side. Don't forget that if you are installing hardwired sconces, you'll need to know what size bed you're getting and exactly where it's going to go during the construction process. If you are going to hardwire sconces, you also want to be pretty sure you won't upgrade to a bigger bed or move it to another wall in the future; you're pretty locked in. If you want to avoid that commitment, you can opt for plug-in sconces or lamps instead.

Finally, you might find it extra cozy to add one more lamp in the room. If your bedroom has space for a sitting area (lucky!), that's a perfect opportunity for a floor lamp or table lamp. Or you can have a table lamp on a dresser.

Once your bedroom is styled and ready to provide some restorative sleep, turn off that overhead light and turn on the bedside sconces and lamps in the room. We promise that seeing your room in that gorgeous cozy light will help you wind down and relax.

Window Coverings

For some people, blocking light from coming in through the windows is really important to a good night's sleep. You can do that with blackout blinds or shades, but soften the space with curtains or drapes. You can even skip the blinds and shades and go straight for blackout curtains.

Architectural Detail

Integrated lighting and wall niches are great if you are short on space for a proper nightstand. We love the juxtaposition of these modern elements with the original wood window details in this bedroom.

Your bedroom is another place in the house that can benefit from some architectural detail. One way to do that is to add picture-frame wall moulding (see page 132) or wainscoting. Another is to build a niche in the wall for shelves. Perhaps an arched entrance, bathroom, or closet door can provide interesting detail. There are many options, but if you can add some architectural detail to the room, it will make it feel like a more special place.

IKEA Dresser Makeover Hack

You don't need to use a dresser from IKEA, but since they have basic pieces at great prices, it's a good place to start if you don't already have one.

TOOLS:

- Tape measure
- Cordless drill and drill bit
- Stapler and staples
- Paintbrush
- Clamps or tape
- Jigsaw
- Miter saw or a fine saw and miter block (Note: If you don't have power tools and don't want to buy any, you can take the drawer fronts to a local lumber yard, and they might cut it for a small fee.)

SUPPLIES:

- Chest of drawers
- Handles (optional; we got ours from House of Antique Hardware)
- Cane webbing (We have to recommend Amazon here—cheap and ships fast! Make sure you order a little extra.)
- Moulding for cabinets (We picked up ¼-inch rounds at Home Depot. Get one on the smaller side so it doesn't feel too large in the drawer.)
- 120-grit sandpaper
- Wood filler
- Wood glue
- Paint
- Pencil

1. DISASSEMBLE THE CHEST OF DRAWERS.

You need to get everything out of the drawers. (When we did ours, we had been hoarding a lot of clothes we don't usually wear in these drawers. So this gave us the perfect opportunity for some early spring cleaning!) Once everything is out, remove the drawers and then take off the existing hardware. If it's IKEA, you won't need any special tools for this—a screwdriver will do. Remove the cabinet fronts, making sure to keep the screws for them!

2. MEASURE, MARK, AND CUT.

Next, cut the holes in the drawer fronts where you'll add the cane webbing. First you want to decide how much border you want around the webbing. You don't want it to be too narrow, otherwise it could leave the drawer too weak. Don't forget that you also still need enough space to attach your new handles too (if you will be using handles).

We went with about 2-inch squares. Measure all the way around and draw the square you'll be cutting out onto the drawer front. Now you're ready to grab your jigsaw and start cutting! (We recommend having a few handy tools around and, if you don't have any, maybe this is a good project to get your toolbox started!) Before you can begin cutting, you'll need to drill a hole inside the area you'll be removing that's big enough to insert your jigsaw blade into. Carefully cut out the square, trying to follow the lines exactly. Don't be discouraged if this is difficult, especially if it's your first time using a jigsaw—you may need a bit of practice. You will also be putting trim around the cut edge to hide any imperfections.

3. SMOOTH THE EDGES AND ATTACH THE MOULDING.

Sand all edges with sandpaper and make sure everything is as smooth as possible. Since the edges you cut will be unfinished (and perhaps with some other imperfections from the cutting), you'll want to hide it with moulding. We used ¼-inch round trim to give it a curved edge detail. You need a miter saw or a miter box to cut the moulding on a 45-degree angle and miter it at the corners. If you've never done this before, our advice is to get an extra couple of lengths of moulding. It's a little tricky and you might have to redo a few of them.

Place the moulding into the cutout to make sure it all fits. If it's not perfect at the miter joints and/or there are small gaps where the moulding meets the cutout, it's okay! We're going to fill it with some wood filler before painting. Glue the mouldings onto the cut

edge and use clamps to hold it into place until it dries. (If you don't have clamps, just hold it in place for about 2 minutes and it should be good from there or use tape to secure it in place.) It should be dry enough to continue after a couple hours, but we waited until the next day, just to be sure.

When it's dried, fill any gaps, uneven cuts, or chips with some wood filler and let it dry before sanding everything so that it's smooth and ready to prime and paint. The wood filler is sandable and paintable, so you won't see these imperfections after it's painted.

4. SAND, PRIME, AND PAINT EVERYTHING.

When you've finished all the cutting, gluing, and filling, it's time to give everything—including the entire dresser—a sanding with some 120-grit sandpaper. We just did ours by hand!

Sanding the surface will roughen it up ever so slightly and provide a good base so the paint sticks. Wipe down everything with a damp rag or paper towel to make sure it's dust-free before painting.

It's a good idea to prime your furniture before painting, but we used a paint-and-primer combination product. Don't forget that you also have to sand between every coat of paint to remove any imperfections and air bubbles and provide more grooves so the next coat of paint sticks.

5. ATTACH THE WEBBING.

When you've finished painting and everything has thoroughly dried (give it a good 24 hours), you can start to update your dresser with cane webbing. Measure and cut your cane webbing, then flip over your drawer fronts and staple a piece of webbing over the opening. (Note: We flattened our webbing a couple days in advance. It comes rolled up and will be hard to work with if it's constantly curling up on you.)

6. ASSEMBLE THE DRAWERS AND ADD HANDLES.

Once it looks like it's back to being a dresser, drill the holes for your new handles. We used these beautiful handles from House of Antique Hardware, which meant that we had to drill two holes into each of the larger drawers and one each in the smaller drawers.

Enjoy your new budget-friendly dresser!

TIP: We could have spent another couple hours measuring exact screw locations for the hardware, but we just used painter's tape to mark the screw holes and then transferred that from the tape onto the drawers! This will save you so much time, and doing it this way is more precise!

Shelves

The final component to a comfortable bedroom is to add a bookshelf or wall shelf for some books and display items. We don't recommend something too big and certainly not with a lot of items, but having even a small place to show a few special things can make your space feel cozier.

Budget Breakdown

There are a lot of places to save in the bedroom. You'll find plenty of affordable and stylish bed frames and headboards to choose from. We even chose to custom upholster a headboard ourselves. It was a fun project, and we love our one-of-a-kind bed! There are also a good number of high-quality and inexpensive mattresses out there. Our favorites are Casper, Nest Bedding, and Allswell.

When it comes to how you dress your bed, you don't have to spend a lot there either. Just make sure to get 300 to 400 thread count sheets and don't forget to layer as we recommended on page 150.

We also love to transform an old piece of furniture into something new. One of our favorite pieces is a plain white IKEA dresser we had for eight years before it was transformed into a totally different piece with a pop of color and cane webbing.

Recipe for Renovating and Designing Your Bedroom Space

1. Remember that everything you do to build your bedroom should focus on creating a relaxing, organized, and comfortable space.

2. Start by making sure there is a good place for your bed to live, even if that means moving other features out of the way.

3. Go with the largest bed that will comfortably fit, and don't forget to leave room for bedside tables.

4. Have a solid, comfortable, and stylish headboard for your bed.

5. Build a primary suite with bedroom, closet, and en suite bathroom.

6. Keep organized by making sure everything has its place, especially your clothes.

7. Give yourself ample closet room even if you have to sacrifice a bit of space in the bedroom itself.

8. Layer your bed with comfortable sheets, duvet, pillows, and throws.

9. Add an area rug to ground your bed and make the room cozy.

10. Consider adding some architectural detail.

11. Create a mood with the lighting.

12. Make the room cozy and comfortable.

What You'll Need

- Furniture: Bed, headboard, dresser, side table, shelves
- Design: Bed linens, pillows, area rug, lamps, window coverings, books and other items to display
- Ample closet space
- En suite bathroom for a primary suite, if possible
- Paint
- Dresser or clothes storage

08

Closet Love

Whether you have room for a large walk-in closet or not, it's easy (and fun!) to get creative with how you lay out your closet and store your items.

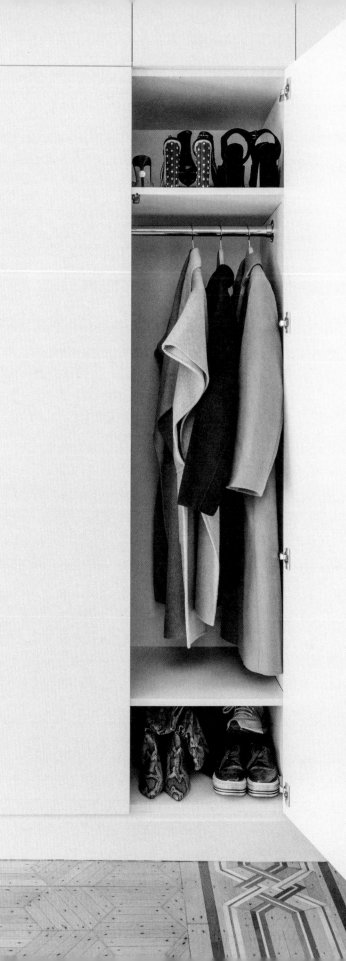

We believe that one of the keys to a comfortable home is an organized closet! Ample closet space is often associated with sprawling suburban homes, but even if you live in a small city apartment, you can make a beautiful, functional space that organizes your clothing perfectly.

Take, for instance, the closet pictured on page 158. It is, in fact, not a closet at all, just a wall of millwork cabinetry that fits snugly in this one-bedroom apartment. You might not be able to tell by looking at this clothing-storage paradise, but this apartment is only 550 square feet! We would argue that the amount of utility this closet serves up is easily equal to the amount of a suburban walk-in closet. The key is organization.

To demonstrate how organization rather than size is what counts, let's go through the exercise of considering how much closet space we can get out of this 12-foot-long millwork closet compared to an average 7 by 6-foot walk-in closet, both of which we'll organize into a haven for your clothes. There are many shapes and sizes of closets out there, and we can't look at them all, but the concepts and comparisons we lay out here can be applied to any closet.

When we look at these three options, the first one, with 14 feet of linear closet space, seems like the winner. It maximizes the amount of space while not creating dead space that's hard to access.

These sleek built-ins add plenty of storage space without adding too much visual clutter to the room. This full-sized coat closet is practically camouflaged into the white walls of this bedroom.

Closet Types

——————

1. Walk-In Closet: A standard 7 by 6-foot walk-in closet can be organized a number of ways. Remember, with a walk-in, some of the space needs to be designated for . . . well, walking. So the amount of actual "closet space" isn't 42 square feet. The most efficient way to lay out this closet would be with two linear rows: In this configuration you will have two linear rows of hanging space, shelves, and drawers, giving us 14 feet total of linear closet space. It leaves 2 feet of walking space in the middle, which is a bit tight but will get the job done.

2. Millwork Closet: The millwork closet pictured at the beginning of this chapter (page 158) takes an entire wall of a bedroom that measures 13 by 16 feet. The closet is 12 feet long, so there is 12 linear feet of closet space. It's 2 feet deep, so it takes up 24 square feet of space from the room. Even though the millwork closet takes up half the space of the walk-in closet described above (24 square feet versus 48 square feet), it offers 85 percent of the closet space. And there's still plenty of space in the room for a queen-size bed and other furniture.

   This example might be extreme, but even when we work with clients designing three- or four-bedroom houses (especially in the historic homes we usually work in), sometimes there just isn't space for a walk-in closet, and that's okay. Also, depending on the size and shape, sometimes the walk-in closet is difficult to configure and offers less storage than a millwork or reach-in.

3. Reach-In Closets: The reach-in closet is probably the most common type. They can be incredibly useful and are relatively easy to squeeze into bedrooms and even hallways. The above example of the millwork closet also applies to reach-in closets; the main difference is that they are built with walls, which does require some additional space. Even if you can have a walk-in closet or a wall of millwork in your primary bedroom, you'll likely need reach-in closets in the other rooms. With the right organization, these closets can offer plenty of storage as well.

   Since reach-in closets are built with walls, this type of closet requires doors. There are several styles that can affect the look and functionality of the closet.

By adding a rug, carving out a space for a vanity, and adding a fun stool, we made this closet feel more like a room itself.

How to Organize a Closet

Now, no matter whether you have a big or small closet, organizing is key to making it as useful as possible. You'll likely want some combination of hanging, shelf, and possibly drawer space. What amount of each is totally up to you. We always work with our clients to understand what kind of closet organization will work best for them. Some people have lots of hanging clothes, others love shelves with stacked folded clothing, while some prefer to tuck things away in drawers. Here are a few things to consider before you get started:

- You'll want a minimum depth of 22 inches for hangers to fit, but 24 inches is preferable.

- There are three standard hanging sizes:

  - Long Hang: 68 inches; for tall coats and long dresses

  - Medium Hang: 56 inches; for long skirts, shorter dresses, shorter coats, cuff-hung pants

  - Short Hang: 42 inches; for shirts, folded pants, suits

- Don't forget to double up the hanging space. Most all men's clothing doesn't need full long hanging height, which takes up a lot of space. Some women's clothing does, but not all, so utilize that space! You can double up the short hang rods to make two levels of hanging clothes.

- Most hanging rods look best with a shelf a few inches over them.

- Utilize all the vertical space you can. Is there room above your closet for additional storage?

All too often closets are finished with a simple shelf and rod. It's the simplest and least expensive way to put your closet to work, but we recommend investing some time and money into organizing your closet well and making it as functional as possible. It might be closed off behind a door, but if it works better, you'll enjoy your bedroom and entire home so much more! Some of our favorite closet organization systems are from IKEA, the Container Store, and California Closets. Within those options, there is something for every style and budget.

A mix of drawers, short hanging, long hanging, and shelves not only makes the most of your space, but helps you stay organized and efficient.

Budget Breakdown

Closet interiors and millwork can get expensive, but you shouldn't have to lack organization just because of budget. There are hacks to build an epic closet at a fraction of the cost of some of the expensive systems. First stop for an inexpensive system can be IKEA. Their Pax system is great and includes all of the bells and whistles the other guys have; we've used it many times. It comes in specific widths and heights, but there have been times we didn't want to be limited. So we have even used kitchen cabinets to create closets. We've done this with IKEA kitchen cabinets and other brands. You can build in shelves and drawers just as you can with closet systems. You can have tall storage or even shorter cabinets stacked on top to utilize height. The only alteration you'll need to make is to buy the rods for hanging separately and then screw them into the side of the interior cabinets. Easy! The closet pictured at the beginning of the chapter (see page 158) was built with inexpensive kitchen cabinets from Boxi by Semihandmade.

Consider double bi-fold doors on a reach-in closet if you're tight on space. They allow you to see everything in your closet at once.

Recipe for Building and Organizing Your Closet

1. Remember that building your space with sufficient and organized closet space is about more than the space itself; it can help your bedroom and entire home work better for you if you can neatly tuck away your clothing.

2. Decide if your space will work best with a walk-in closet, reach-in closet, or millwork closet.

3. Start by considering what combination of closet storage would work best for you: hanging, shelves, and/or drawers.

4. Don't forget to double up hanging space as most clothing doesn't need that much height.

5. Shelves and drawers can also be very useful and a great use of space in a closet.

6. Invest in a good organization system that offers flexibility to design your closet to work best for you.

What You'll Need

- Doors or millwork
- A system that fits into your budget and offers the flexibility you need
- Hanging space
- Shelf space
- Drawers
- Hooks

09

Door and Moulding Love

The original trim in this home had such rich texture and detail. A medium dark stain highlights the depth of the trim and makes the windows and doors a focal point in this bright front room.

The icing on the cake in your home is the moulding and trim. It's one of your best opportunities to add charm and detail. Unless you're building a modern, minimalist box, you will want baseboards, door and window casings, and/or crown moulding. Not all are necessary depending on your home, but very few people will skip them completely. For the type of homes we typically work in, the more the merrier! We even take very special care to save historic trim and moulding and restore them back to their original beauty. So whether you're restoring a historic home, adding some detail to a newer home, or going ultramodern, let's talk all the trim details.

In a historic home, it's all about restoring and elevating those original features, like door trim. Don't be afraid of a few dark spots and imperfections—they add to the home's character.

Doors

Your home will have a lot of interior doors and a few exterior doors. Style and material will vary between them. Doors consist of a door slab itself, a frame that the door will operate within, hinges and hardware, and the casing.

Doors and mouldings literally live right next to one another. Your choice for one might even inform your choice for the other. They should definitely be in the same style, they are typically painted or finished the same color, and they are often even made out of the same material.

You'll likely need to order your doors first because they will be installed before the moulding.

INTERIOR DOORS

Your interior doors are a very important part of your renovation. They help separate your rooms and living spaces and offer privacy when needed, but since they are a part of every room, they help define the style of your home as well.

1. Door Styles: Doors come in a variety of styles. What you choose will have a big effect on the overall aesthetic of your home. A flat slab (no panel) door offers a more modern feel, while a door with panels, mullions, and sticking will be more traditional. In between there are Shaker panel doors that give you some detail but with clean lines. If you want interior doors with a bit more character, Shaker doors with various panels can be an inexpensive option. For this, we like to use five-panel Shaker doors, which keep the cost down compared to more detailed paneled doors.

2. Door Swing: One of the biggest (and often overlooked) considerations for buying doors is the door swing (the direction in which the door opens). Typically doors swing into a room and toward a wall; the door should open toward the perpendicular wall so that you have a view of the room as you open it. If a door is in the middle of a wall, then it's up to you which way it swings; just make sure you put the light switch on the side of the door opposite the direction it swings, or you'll have to close it to reach the switch (we have done that, and let us tell you we wish we would have checked one more time!).

   - Right-hand swing: If you are entering a room, stand with your back toward the side with the hinges. If the door swings to your right, it's a right-hand swing door.

This Shaker panel door combines modern lines with a classic look. The four panels create depth, shadow, and variety.

- **Left-hand swing:** If you are entering a room, stand with your back to the side with the hinges. If the door swings to your left it's a left-hand swing door.

  To complicate things just a bit more, there is also inswing and outswing to consider. If you stand outside the room or house and you push the door open, that's inswing; if you pull it open, that's outswing. What we just covered are inswing doors, which are more common inside a home; see page 175 for exterior doors. It sounds like a lot, but believe us, you'll want to check multiple times that all of your doors are ordered with the correct swing!

3. **Materials:** Interior doors can be solid or hollow core. Please, for the sake of all that is design holy, use only solid-core doors. The hollow-core doors are light and flimsy feeling. Solid-core doors can be solid wood or have a core that's a man-made material, like MDF. The latter can be less expensive and perfectly fine in most scenarios. You'll want to know if you are painting or finishing your doors before choosing the material.

4. **Door Sizes:** Doors do come in custom sizes, but you'll probably be working with standard sizes. There are also likely local building codes for minimums of some door sizes. The typical thickness of interior doors is 1⅜ inches or 1¾ inches. The most common heights are 80 inches and 84 inches; however, some homes (especially historic homes) do have taller doors. The width of your doors is what can vary the most. Standard sizes increase in about 2-inch increments, starting at 24 inches and going up to 36 inches. You will want the rough opening to be about 2½ inches larger than the door itself. So for a 30 by 84-inch door, you will want a rough opening of 32½ by 86½ inches. You may also be replacing doors in their existing frames. In that case, you'll want to make sure the door fits the frame exactly.

5. **Door Hinges:** The most common type of hinge is the butt hinge, which is likely the type you'll use on all of your doors. You can see this hinge on the interior side of the door. In some circumstances, however, you may want the hinge to be concealed on both sides of the door. If so, you'll want to use a concealed hinge like a soss hinge or a pivot hinge.

6. **Closet Doors:** If your closet has a single door, it will likely operate just like your other interior doors, and it will almost certainly swing out and into the room (not into the closet), unless it is a massive walk-in closet. You will likely have some reach-in closets with double doors as well. (See also page 162.)

EXTERIOR DOORS

Exterior doors have many of the same characteristics as interior doors. However, there are also some differences. First of all, the swing of a door is almost always viewed from the exterior. It can be very easy to mistakenly assess the swing of the door from the interior. Inswing and outswing become even more important. Some exterior doors do swing out. If you remember when we talked about door swing (page 172), it can feel the opposite. For instance, if your door is outswing (which means if you are standing outside you pull it open) and you pull it open to your right, it's actually a left-hand outswing door. When in doubt stand with your back on the doorframe with the hinges, and you will see that the door swings to your left.

Many exterior doors have glass, and when they do, it's often referred to as a lite. Doors come in many different configurations of lites, such as full lite, half lite, top lite, and sidelites. The window above the door is called a transom.

The material and thickness of exterior doors are often different than interior, because they need to do a much better job standing up to the elements and insulating your home. Most exterior doors are solid wood or fiberglass, and they are at least 1¾ inches thick and up to 2¼ inches.

HARDWARE

The hardware you choose for your doors can also help define the style of your home. On one side, there are the hinges and on the other side is the doorknob or lever. You'll want the finishes to match. You can get privacy hardware (that gives you the ability to lock it) or passage hardware (that has no locking functionality). Another common hardware type is dummy or fixed, which is only a knob or lever and has no functionality other than giving you something to hold and pull open. If you do use dummy or fixed hardware, you'll also want some sort of mechanism, like a ball or magnetic catch, so that the door stays closed.

Door hardware and locks install on the door in two main ways: either mortised into the door or on a standard cylindrical bore. Mortised locks are usually found in older homes and doors and vary per the actual hardware. So if you have a mortised hardware, no other mortised hardware can be installed in your door, requiring the more difficult preparation for the lock installation to be done by a skilled carpenter. You will also need the specifications of the hardware you are installing to make the lock prep. Modern doors usually have a standard 2¼-inch cylindrical bore. Many doors can easily come with the bore (or double bore for an exterior door with a dead bolt) already done for you. Anyone can easily install cylindrical hardware with a screwdriver, and it can be swapped out for other standard hardware anytime you like.

Moulding

We love moulding. Not many things can transform a space the way moulding can. It can also be one of the most difficult design elements to master. When we first started designing and renovating houses, we found mouldings frustrating because there was just so much we felt we didn't know. There were so many times that we just wanted to take a class on moulding and trim! Now that we have learned so much (but feel like there is still more to learn!), we love it. So, forgive us if we go into some deep detail and make this the class we wish we could have taken!

As beautiful as mouldings can make a space, they also serve an important function. They protect sensitive areas on a wall (think about how scuffed your baseboards get and imagine how the walls would look like without them!), and they also cover awkward places where materials come together, like where the hardwood floors meet the walls.

Let's start at the bottom and work our way up.

BASEBOARDS

Baseboards can be as simple as squared-off flat stock or can be as ornate as a multipiece build-up. The height of your ceilings will usually determine how high they go. With a standard 8-foot ceiling height, you will want your baseboards to be 4 to 6 inches high. With taller ceilings of 9 to 10 feet, your baseboards should be 7 to 9 inches tall. With extra-tall ceilings or if you just want an extra-tall base, you can even go up to 10 or 11 inches.

Taller and more ornate baseboards have a more traditional feel and will fit nicely in a historic home. They also will usually consist of multiple pieces, with a flat stock at the bottom and a base cap at the top. The base cap will be the more ornate of the two.

DOOR AND WINDOW CASINGS

Door casing and window casing are the mouldings that surround your doors and windows. Similar concepts to baseboard size apply. A bigger casing is usually associated with a more traditional or historic home. You also might want a bigger casing on a bigger door or window. The larger casings are also sometimes made of multiple pieces of trim. A typical casing size is 3 to 4 inches.

WALL MOULDING, PANELING, AND WAINSCOTING

This is where the fun starts! (If you weren't already having fun.) Wall moulding and paneling can really give your space a ton of character. It can also be an inexpensive upgrade. The simplest type is small pieces of moulding installed in squares on the walls. Some people call it picture-frame moulding. It's usually a wood moulding, and we have even used pieces of baseboard base cap for it. The keys to making it look great are proportion and consistency. Here are some popular configurations.

Wainscoting can be a bit more expensive and complicated. It comes in many varieties, from simple Shaker profile to a more ornate paneling. It consists of a thin, flat plywood panel base with rails and stiles and other pieces of moulding. Depending on how ornate you want it to be, you can use more or less moulding.

You can set a room's tone by installing wainscoting around an entire room, but you also can use it in small doses as a feature.

The picture frame moulding in this primary suite was easy to install and helps carry the historic look of the home into this otherwise modern bedroom.

Have Fun with Interior Doors with Glass

We like adding a bit of character to a room by using an interior door with glass. One of our favorite ways to do this is to get a vintage door that already has glass or to add glass by cutting out the top panel. We like the glass at the top because it reminds us of an old office or school door. It's a fun DIY project, or you can have a woodworker help with some of the door alterations. However you do it, it's a great way to put some personal style into your home.

STEP 1: Find the door.

Start by finding a vintage door or getting a new door with an open panel at the top. Some new doors come with glass, but we have found that we like to source our own glass to give it the right look. If we are buying a vintage door, we look for one that is the closest to the size we need, if not the exact size. If it's a new door, then you can get the right size for the opening.

STEP 2: Alter the door (or the opening) to size and prepare it for glass.

Once you have your door picked out, you need to make sure it will fit perfectly. If you bought a new door, it should be the correct size, but if it's a vintage door, it might need some alterations. You have two options to make it fit. You can build the opening to fit the door or you can alter the door to fit the opening. Many of the vintage doors we get need some alteration. This might be where you want to find a woodworker (or your contractor) to help. They can cut the door down or remove the stiles and rails (the vertical and horizonal framing for the door) and replace them if needed. Some of the vintage doors we get have solid panels at the top, which are cut out and a small piece of trim is added to hold the glass in place.

STEP 3: Get your glass.

After our door is ready, we measure the open top panel for the size of the glass. We go to a local glass shop that has a variety of options of specialty glass, like glass with chicken wire or reeded glass. There are also salvage stores that sell vintage glass if you really want it to have a lot of character. We provide the measurements, they cut it to size, and we walk out with the piece of glass in hand.

STEP 4: Install your glass.

Installing glass is very easy once the door is prepped for it. You just remove the little piece of moulding that is in place to hold the glass (when a door is prepped for glass, the moulding is usually just tacked into place so that it can be easily removed for the glass installation). Insert the glass and then nail the moulding in place with finishing nails.

STEP 5: Add the final touches.

To finish it off, we either paint or stain the door. Adding a pop of color or a classic black paint will really make it a special feature. Finally, to make it fun, we often add decal lettering to the door. For instance, in our home we put in a vintage door with glass for our guest bathroom, and the lettering on it reads *WC*.

Creating a semi-custom door is a great way to amplify the design flow of the room. When you open this vintage-inspired W.C. door, you enter a completely vintage-inspired space.

CROWN MOULDING

Crown molding also varies in size and profile. An ultramodern house may not have crown moulding at all. A traditional or historic home may be defined by it. Depending on the style of your home, you can go big or go minimal. Just as with baseboards, the height of your ceilings is one of the biggest determining factors. Crown mouldings are measured in three dimensions. Imagine a triangle with the 90-degree edges on the ceiling and wall and the other edge at a 45-degree angle across. The wall edge is the height, the ceiling edge is the projection, and the 45-degree edge is the face. It can be hard to visualize, so we recommend getting some sample pieces and putting them up in the room to get a feel for the scale. Here are some examples:

Unlike baseboards and casings that are almost always wood, crown comes in a few different materials.

1. Plaster: Traditional and historic crown mouldings are often made of plaster. These are the mouldings that make you say *wow* when you enter a room. Since plaster is moulded into shape, it offers a lot of flexibility in creating coves (the curved part of the crown moulding) and details. It can be difficult to replicate historic plaster crown moulding with wood because you don't usually achieve the plaster's deep coves when using wood. The drawback to plaster moulding is that it is typically more expensive because a highly skilled plaster worker needs to create it.

2. Wood: Most modern crown moulding is made of wood. There are many profiles and styles available; however, as mentioned, it doesn't always do a great job of replicating plaster. Wood mouldings are inexpensive and easier to install.

3. Composite material: There are many composite and man-made materials on the market for crown moulding as well. They can be lightweight and inexpensive. Since crown moulding isn't placed in a part of the home you are likely to touch, this type of lightweight material can be used successfully. And because it's moulded into shape, some do a good job of replicating plaster better than wood.

The height of your ceilings and style of home can help determine what size crown mouldings to use.

8-foot ceilings: A one-piece smaller crown about 2½ to 6 inches tall will be fine.

9-foot ceilings: The crown moulding can be 3 to 7½ inches, plus the addition of a picture-frame moulding (see page 132). When using wood, these larger crowns are often "built-up" using a combination of two or more moulding profiles.

10-foot-plus ceilings: A minimum of 4 inches, while formal spaces will need a crown of at least 9 inches. In some cases, you will want a full entablature (cornice plus picture mould) that's up to 24 inches in height.

OTHER MOULDINGS

There are many different types of moulding out there, but here are a few more that you might want to know about:

1. Picture rail moulding: This is a single piece of moulding that runs several inches below the crown. It's used in more historical and traditional homes, and as its name suggests, it was used to hang art so nails would not damage the plaster walls.

2. Chair rail moulding: Similar to picture rail moulding, chair rail is a single piece of moulding that runs around a room about 36 to 48 inches from the floor. It's also found in more traditional homes and originally was used to protect the walls as chairs are pulled out and pushed in to a table.

3. Shoe moulding: A small piece of moulding installed at the bottom of your baseboard. It's usually used when floors are replaced without removing the baseboard and then the small gap needs to be covered.

Budget Breakdown

The doors and trim you put in your home don't need to be expensive. If you're painting the interior trim, you can get lower-cost primed pine or primed MDF. Either will do a great job.

If you want interior doors with a bit more detail but you don't have the budget for doors that have ornate panels, try a simple Shaker profile on a door with multiple panels. We like to use five-panel Shaker doors to give the design a richer feel.

Wall moulding is an inexpensive purchase that brings in a lot of character. It's also a great DIY project that anyone can do!

If your house has historic plaster crown mouldings that are in bad shape, you may have found that repairing them is a budget buster! As much as we adore plaster mouldings and do everything we can to save them, including expensive repairs, we understand that sometimes the budget is just not there. Even though wood mouldings are much less expensive, wood does not do a good job of replicating the look of plaster and therefore isn't an option for us. Fortunately, there are some synthetic crown mouldings on the market that can look just like plaster ones once installed and painted at the cost and ease of installing wood moulding. We like the options from Orac Decor and Ekena Millwork.

For this brownstone parlor, we refreshed the existing trim paint in this pristine white that carries throughout the room. Here, the trim and mouldings are more subtle, but still stand out.

Recipe for Doors and Mouldings

DOORS

1. Remember that doors are functional but can also determine the style and look of your home.

2. Start by measuring your rough opening (if you are replacing a door and frame) or frame size (if you are just replacing the door slab).

3. Decide what style door you will be using (no panel, Shaker, panel with sticking, etc.).

4. Decide which type of hardware (cylindrical or mortised) and hinges (butt hinges or concealed hinges) you will be using.

5. Decide what material your doors will be. One of the biggest considerations is whether you are staining/finishing or painting the doors.

MOULDING

1. The size and profile of your mouldings are determined by the height of your ceilings, size of the space, and style of the house.

2. Start at the bottom and work your way up.

3. Baseboard height is determined by the height of your ceilings. Use taller baseboards for taller ceilings and shorter for lower ceilings.

4. Decide if you'll be adding any wall moulding or wainscoting.

5. Choose a crown moulding that suits the style of your house and the height of your ceilings.

What You'll Need

- Door slab and frame
- Door hardware
- Hinges
- Saddle or threshold (usually for exterior doors)
- Baseboards
- Crown moulding
- Other mouldings: show moulding, wall moulding, wainscoting, picture rail moulding

10

Floor Love

Finding a beautiful,
detailed wood floor in
an old home is such
a treat. The delicate
inlay in this hardwood
border was worth
every minute of repair
and restoration!

You might not initially realize that your flooring is one of the most prominent materials in your home. It may even be the single material that carries throughout many of your rooms. For that reason, your flooring choice has the ability to set the tone for your entire home.

The contrasting colors and patterns of this parlor floor are the first thing you notice in this parlor. Floors aren't just practical, they truly have a transformative power in the design of any room.

Wood Floors

The king of all flooring materials is undoubtedly wood. It's been used for centuries, and if it ain't broke, don't fix it! But that isn't the end of the story, there are lots of options.

There are two main types of wood flooring: solid wood and engineered wood. Solid wood flooring is exactly what it sounds like: A wood plank is cut from one piece of wood. Its biggest advantage is that it can be sanded and restored many times over its lifetime. If we need to replace flooring in a historic home, we enjoy putting in solid wood floors because that's what would have originally been there.

Engineered wood flooring looks very similar to solid wood flooring on the surface, but the visible layer is a relatively thin layer of hardwood over a core of layers of high-quality plywood. If this is a new concept for you, you might initially reason that solid wood must be better, and we wouldn't blame you! But the construction of the layers of plywood can create a big advantage over solid wood. Wood tends to want to move around as it expands and contracts in different temperature and humidity conditions; engineered flooring is less likely to shift with these changing environmental conditions. The biggest disadvantage is that because of the thinner layer of surface material, you can only sand and refinish it once or twice in its lifetime. (Though, truth be told, most people very rarely sand their floors. Maybe once every ten years, if even.) So your engineered floors will last a very long time. The point here is that there is no reason to shy away from engineered wood floors with a belief that solid wood floors are better simply because they are . . . well, solid wood.

UNFINISHED OR PREFINISHED?

You can purchase your wood flooring unfinished so that it can be finished on-site or prefinished from the factory and ready to enjoy. Unfinished wood flooring is raw wood that needs to be sealed and finished to protect it. It can also be stained any color or tone that you would like. If you're matching existing flooring or other wood features in your home, you might want to have this level of customization. The most common type of flooring finish is water-based polyurethane. It's what we most often use. In fact, we love getting unfinished hardwood floors (usually white oak) and simply finishing them with a matte, clear (no stain) water-based polyurethane. You get to see the wood in its natural tone, while it's protected for years to come.

Prefinished wood floors come in many different colors, textures, and tones. They can even be hand-distressed for a rustic or vintage look. You have a high level of customization with prefinished floors since they are finished in a factory or shop by a team that worked very hard on the process to get a specific look. It's

For this intricate floor medallion, we went with a clear, matte finish to elevate the natural beauty of the different types of wood.

often difficult for your contractor crew/floor installer to achieve the same specific finishes on-site with unfinished wood. Some prefinished flooring can get very expensive because of the time and effort that goes into it.

The most common type of hardwood flooring is oak, either white or red. We prefer the tones in white oak. Some other species to consider are walnut, maple, ash, and pine.

This home had a challenging position for natural light, so we chose a clean and crisp light-toned hardwood for the floor. The consistent flooring throughout ties the spaces together.

Wood Species

Oak: The most common type of wood for hardwood floors, oak is readily available and affordable. It has a medium to high hardness rating, which makes it very durable. Its natural tone is a light caramel color, but it can be stained lighter or darker.

Walnut: Walnut floors have an unmistakable look. They are a dark, rich color with beautiful graining. They will definitely make a statement in a home as an alternative to oak, which mostly blends into the background. Walnut can be expensive and is on the softer side, so it's not as durable as other species.

Maple: Maple is a common wood species. There are many variations of it, so it tends to differ a lot in terms of price, quality, hardness, and grain pattern. Be sure to get a sample to make certain it's what you're looking for. Maple flooring is typically harder than oak, so it's extremely durable. In fact, it's the type of hardwood most commonly used in bowling alleys!

Ash: Ash is less expensive than oak but has some similarities, which makes it a good alternative. It also has the same hardness as oak, so it is durable. It's easy to install, stain, and refinish. It also has a unique grain that is comparable to oak. Ash wood floors are known particularly for their light color.

Pine: Pine floors are very common in older homes. It was available and easy to mill because it's a softer wood, but that makes it less durable and prone to scrapes and dings in houses. Many of the old homes we work in have original pine wood plank floors that act as both a subfloor and a floor surface. We love to refinish them, because there is no better way to honor the history of the original floors, but because softer wood takes a beating over the course of many years, the result is often a rustic look.

GRADES OF HARDWOOD FLOORING

Most people don't realize that there are different grades of hardwood flooring. Especially for oak flooring, there are three main grades: select, number 1 common, and number 2 common. Select is generally considered the highest category, as it has the least color variation and the fewest knots. Because of that, it can cost more. Number 1 has more color variation and some occasional knots, while number 2 has even more color variation and knots. Sometimes, number 2 is called "character grade" or "cabin grade" wood. This grade has the lowest cost, but that isn't the only reason it might work for you. The variation, knots, and character might fit right in with your design!

There is one more big decision you may encounter when you buy your hardwood floors: the types of cut. There are three basic cuts of lumber for hardwood flooring: plain sawn, quarter sawn, and rift sawn. Each cut results in a unique look and affects the cost of material.

1. Plain Sawn: Plain sawn is the most common cut of lumber used in hardwood flooring. It's simply making parallel cuts through the log. This gives the plank a very distinct "cathedral grain," which basically means that you can see the rings of the grain. There is very little waste produced, so it's the most affordable.

2. Quarter Sawn: Quarter sawn lumber is produced when the log is cut into four quarters (hence the name), then each quarter is flat sawn. This results in a more linear grain pattern without the "cathedral" effect. In oak, this produces a flecking or ray in the grain, which can be a striking design choice. Since this type of cut produces more waste, the cost is higher than plain sawn lumber.

3. Rift Sawn: By far, rift sawn lumber is both the most expensive and the least common option on the market. The log is milled perpendicular to the growth rings. This produces a linear, straight grain with a clean, consistent look. This method produces the most waste, significantly increasing the cost of the material. Rift sawn boards are either cut as complements to previously cut quarter sawn boards or purposely sawn using the rift method. This results in a linear grain pattern that has no flecking.

HARDWOOD FLOOR SIZING

You will want to choose a width and length of plank for your floors. Depending on the look and installation technique, you might want a narrower plank or a wider one. Traditional and historic inlay floors and parquet floors are often made with narrow plank boards about 1 to 2 inches wide. If you are laying your floor in a herringbone or chevron pattern, you might want a board width in the range of 3 to 5 inches and likely 18 to 24 inches long. If you are laying your floors as standard planks, you can choose a wider 7- to 10-inch plank and up.

You might be focused on the width of your hardwood floor planks because it's the more obvious feature, but keep in mind that you will also want to think about the length. Most hardwood floors are laid with varying size planks to create a randomized pattern. Usually the longer the plank, the more expensive it will be. We recommend no shorter than 2 feet long and going up to 7 to 10 feet. Be sure not to have too many short planks, and definitely try not to install them too close to one another. It's a telltale sign of a cheap floor when we see too many short planks close to one another.

INSTALLATION

Installation techniques will vary based on the type of hardwood floor you choose. Many are manufactured with tongue-and-groove edges that make it easier to align. Some engineered flooring is manufactured with click-together edges that lock in place. Solid wood floors are often nailed in place as long as you are installing over a wood subfloor. Engineered flooring is often glued down and sometimes, in the case of click-together flooring, it floats with no glue or nails. You'll want to ask the flooring supplier what their recommendation is and, of course, ask your flooring installer what they recommend based on the conditions.

Tile

There are many shapes and sizes of tile available. The shape you choose contributes as much to the design as the color.

While hardwood is the most common material we see used for floors, tile is definitely second. Even in homes that have hardwood floors, you'll often find tile in areas that may deal with wet conditions where wood won't hold up. It's common (and often necessary) in bathrooms as well as kitchens and entryways. It can even run throughout the house, and it is easy to clean. You'll see it in warm climates where it might be important to keep things cool.

TILE SIZE

One of the decisions you'll make when you are choosing tile is the size. You might be drawn to the serene spa-like effect of a large-format (24 by 24 inches or larger) tile. Or maybe you prefer the traditional look of a mosaic tile, which is often about 1 by 1 inch and sheeted (on a mesh sheet usually about 12 by 12 inches, so you don't need to install thousands of tiny tiles!). We love the old-world look of a mosaic tile but also like the modern effect of a square tile in a matte pop of color.

Tile Types

Ceramic Tile: Ceramic tile is one of the most common types of tile because it's suitable for many applications and comes in hundreds of styles that can fit any design. It's durable and can work in any room in the house.

Porcelain: Like ceramic tile, porcelain tile is durable and comes in many colors, styles, and designs. It even has the ability to emulate the look of natural stone, brick, or wood but without any of the maintenance or upkeep. Porcelain can even be used outdoors, as it will not freeze, fade, or crack. We often use it on decks and patios to create an outdoor room effect.

Cement: Cement tile has been around for centuries and is often associated with Moroccan or Spanish style. It is experiencing a bit of a comeback in interior design and usually comes in many different patterns and colors. The drawback is that cement is extremely porous. It needs to be sealed well and can be prone to staining and discoloration.

Natural Stone: There are several types of natural stone that can make quite a statement in your home. Marble and travertine are two of our favorites. They are beautiful but a bit more costly and can be susceptible to staining and weathering, so they are best used in low traffic areas (unless you might enjoy the process of the patina like we do!).

Carpet

You might find that carpet is the best option for certain areas of your home, but we'll be honest, we would use it sparingly. While carpet has its place, we wouldn't suggest wall-to-wall carpet throughout your home. It requires a lot of maintenance and can collect just about anything and everything over the years. For that reason, limiting it to areas like bedrooms is probably best. Its pros are that it creates a cozy feel and does a good job absorbing sound. For us, area rugs have the same qualities as carpet and can be changed more easily, so we tend to use them on top of hardwood floors rather than installing wall-to-wall carpeting.

Heated Floors

If you live in a cold climate, heated floors can be the ultimate luxury! If you are already installing a new floor, it can be a manageable upgrade, especially in smaller areas like bathrooms. A heating element is installed before the floor goes in. It can be electric or hydronic (if your home has a hot water radiator system). It might even be possible to install heated floors throughout your home in lieu of a traditional heating system.

Measure Well

It's important to make sure you get enough flooring to finish the job, but you also don't want to waste money on piles of extra. If it's a rectangular-shaped room, then it's easy! A bedroom that's 12 by 10 feet will need 120 square feet of flooring. If not, try separating the space into two rectangles or, for very oddly shaped rooms, find the largest rectangle and estimate the remaining odd area the best you can. Once you have the square footage for each room, add them all up. Then there is one more step. Almost all hardwood flooring comes with planks that you might not want to use for various reasons. Maybe they are too short or blemished. Also, any flooring material will have to be cut around some places, such as the edges. All of this produces waste, so you'll want to have overage to account for it. You should plan for at least 10 percent overage, but if there is a long lead time or a special installation (like herringbone or chevron), we would recommend 15 percent overage to be sure you have enough. The last step is to multiply the total square footage by the amount you want as overage and add the two together.

FOLLOWING PAGE:
We chose a white oak floor in a herringbone pattern from Stuga to add character and charm in this modern loft renovation.

Budget Breakdown

Flooring is one of the materials you need in a large quantity for your home, so it can add up. Prefinished hardwood and handmade tiles can be very expensive. Our recommendation to keep things in check is to use unfinished hardwood flooring and finish it on-site. Flooring suppliers tend to buy it in bulk and keep it in stock. If you want to find a great deal, call a few local suppliers and ask them what unfinished flooring they have a lot of at a low cost. Chances are they will have stock of white or red oak in 4-, 5-, or 6-inch-wide planks. If you want a more distressed look at a low cost, get plain-sawn character-grade flooring. Talk to your contractor about distressing it further if they have that skill. If you want a cleaner look, get a select grade, which will come at a premium price. Plain sawn will be cheaper, but if you prefer rift and quarter sawn, check pricing and compare. As long as you are okay with any of those options, you can likely get a good deal. We prefer to pay around $7 to 8 per square foot for a decent quality select grade oak floor. Keep in mind everything we talked about regarding length of boards and the type of cut (see page 193).

Combining different tiles in the same space can be a budget-friendly way to incorporate stand-out tile with more standard designs.

Tile can get very expensive; there are amazing handmade and bespoke tile companies making some gorgeous options. Our suggestion to keep the costs down is to use that type of tile sparingly and pair it with something inexpensive from larger tile suppliers like TileBar or Nemo Tile.

Recipe for Choosing and Ordering Floors

1. Don't forget that your floors might just be the largest surface material in your house, so don't underestimate the amount they can contribute to the overall look.

2. Consider the general feel you want your space to have and what will be the most functional flooring. Keep in mind upkeep and how the material will age.

3. Decide what type of flooring is best for you: wood, tile, stone, or carpet.

4. Choose between various species of wood or types of tile.

5. With the help of the flooring supplier and installer, decide what installation method will be used.

6. Measure your space to figure out the square footage.

7. Don't forget to account for waste and add 10 to 15 percent overage to your order.

What You'll Need

- Tape measure
- Pencil and paper or some other way to keep track of the square footage of each room
- Square footage of space, including overage
- Flooring material: wood, tile, stone, carpet, or other material
- Nails or glue depending on installation method (sometimes supplied by installer)
- Qualified flooring installer

11

Window and Exterior Love

The facade of this former carriage house-turned-junk-shop is now clean and contemporary while still calling back to its historic roots. See the before shot on page 23.

Y ou know what they say about first impressions! The curb appeal of your home says a lot about what someone might find on the inside. It isn't all about looks though; your windows and exterior doors are a first line of defense when it comes to weatherproofing and efficiency.

A black satin paint adorns this brownstone's original entry doors, giving it an elegant, timeless look.

Updating a Facade

Our own home renovation journey started by walking around our favorite neighborhoods, gawking at the beautiful exteriors, and peeking in the windows as we went by. The inviting and stately facades and a small glimpse through the windows drew us into the story of the homes. It made us want to have one of our own. So, it goes without saying that creating that type of experience for our home and the ones we work on is important to us. Is your fixer-upper house not looking so inviting right now? Let's fix it!

FRONT DOOR

Your front door says something about who lives there. It's a great opportunity to set the design tone for your home. It's probably the single most important feature on the front of your house that invites people in! How do you choose one that's going to say, "Come on in—it's even better on the inside!"

Since you usually want to draw attention to your front door, we like to make it pop. This doesn't always mean painting it a bright color, but you better believe that sometimes it does! You want the front door to stand out, so make it contrast. Go ahead and paint it that bright shade of red or yellow or blue or green. But if you want something a little more subtle, a beautiful natural wood or even black can pop against a light-colored facade.

One example is the white-brick home on page 200. The window shutters, garage door, and cornice are all black, while the front door is a stunning and dramatic caramel-toned white oak. It's a pop of warmth against the otherwise cooler black-and-white color scheme. We feel this front door introduces the story of what's inside much more than a black door that matches the rest of the trim would have.

We like a front door with glass. It adds character to the door and lets natural light into the entryway. But privacy is important, too, so you can opt for a top light (like the door on the white-brick home on page 200), a half light, or even obscured glass.

There are many designs for doors out there. Choosing a door with some panels can add character, but we would avoid dated-looking dark wood tones or ornate glass.

HARDWARE

Don't underestimate the impact your front door hardware can have on the overall look. Often just painting the door and changing the hardware can sufficiently upgrade the exterior. We like to use a modern hardware set even on a historic home, because we enjoy that juxtaposition, but sometimes a historic-inspired set is called for. Our advice is to avoid anything too ornate. Keep it simple and clean.

HOUSE NUMBERS

If there is one thing on the front of your house that communicates with the outside world, it's the house numbers. You're literally starting a conversation with potential guests. So make it upbeat and interesting! We almost always go with something modern looking, again creating a juxtaposition with a historic home. Make sure the size is large enough to see from the street, and choose a modern, streamlined font that people can easily read. You'll also want to make sure that the numbers contrast to whatever they are mounted on.

CLEAN IT UP

Yes, this one is a no-brainer. Many times you can liven up your home's facade just with a thorough power washing. Years of grime might be making the exterior look dingy, and cleaning it off, along with the other updates, can complete the look.

PAINT

A fresh coat of paint can make the front of your home look brand-new, regardless of whether you decide to change the color. It also protects wood surfaces from the elements and prevents costly repair jobs down the line. Choose a contrasting color for trim items (like shutters and doors), and feel free to go bold; just keep it tasteful and mindful of your surroundings. In some neighborhoods, it might be common to paint a home or its facade trim in a bright pastel color, and if that's where you are, go crazy, but in most neighborhoods, things are a bit more subtle. You might still want to stand out, but choose something that knocks it out of the park while not being too far out in left field.

OUTDOOR LIGHTING

You'll want your home's facade to be inviting day and night. Just like the inside, lighting can set the mood. First and foremost, ample front porch and door lighting is key. Make sure there is bright-enough light overhead so you can easily find your keys and get them in the door! If it's not an option to install overhead lights, then go with wall-mounted or even a post light near the door. Choose a light that makes a statement and tells a story the same way you might do inside. For instance, a clean-lined modern light might say, "Yes, our home is stately but we are fun and unexpected too."

Pay attention to lighting your newly installed house numbers. You'll want people to see them clearly as they approach your home at night. It can also be a dramatic touch. Consider an uplight or downlight here and other places on the facade. A few strategically placed fixtures to light up the outside can make the house seem inviting and impressive.

Walkway or sidewalk lighting can light the way and create a cozy feel. Place path lights in the ground or in planters about every 4 to 6 feet on the side of your sidewalk. As a final touch, light the landscaping! Place uplights in the trees and light the flowerbeds to really make your home a nighttime feast for the eyes.

LANDSCAPING

Landscaping that's too mature and overgrown can give your home a closed-off feel. If you have overgrown greenery, cut it back to a more appropriate size, so that your home is clearly seen, and fit in some new plants as well. If something is too big and dominating the landscaping, don't be afraid to free yourself and remove it. Keep things simple. Don't mix too many different colors and styles. Pick one or two accent colors and be careful not to select too many shades of green. It will feel more cohesive and well thought out if you repeat the same few kinds of plants and colors. If your home is taller (two stories or more), bring the plantings out farther from the home (up to about 8 feet) so that they are in the same scale as the house. Think about lining the walkway and even adding some sidewalk or street-side plantings as well.

To add beauty and additional shade to a front yard, carefully place accent trees between the street and the house. Trees give your front yard and home a look of permanence and make a lasting impression. Think about using something that flowers or changes colors with the seasons to keep it interesting year-round!

BIGGER FACADE PROJECTS

Your facade might need a little bit more than a dressing up. If your home lacks a substantial entrance, for instance, think about adding a front porch. If the facade material is looking drab, change it to something fab. Adding brick can make your home more stately and elegant. Wood cladding or standing seam siding (vertical siding panels) can provide a modern aesthetic. Cement or stucco can give you a durable and clean look. Limestone or brownstone can create a stately and historic feel.

It's important to remember that making a change to your exterior can be an extension of the design inside. There is a terra-cotta-tiled deck off this kitchen, which complements this room's aesthetic.

Stand back from your home and notice its proportions. Does the entrance need more weight? Or does either side throw off the symmetry? It's often worth changing the overall proportions of a building. This might be done by adding or enlarging a front porch, or you might need to build up or out. Will a roof gable create more interest, symmetry, and substance? Will adding more or larger windows not only create balance on the exterior but more light for the interior? Don't be afraid to go big. If you're doing a major renovation, you'll want to give the front exterior of your home as much attention as you give the interior.

Windows

Changing your home's windows might be one of the most important items on your renovation to-do list. They are a feature that carries through to likely every room in the house. They play a big part in your home's interior and exterior aesthetics as well as having one of the most vital roles in its efficiency.

So, if you've decided to invest in new windows for your home—congratulations! Now it's time to tackle the details. Understanding the parts that make up the anatomy of a window will help avoid confusion and give you a leg up while shopping for windows. Understanding new construction versus replacement windows will help you order the right thing. Knowing the meaning of balances, sashes, and lifts will help you understand how a window operates. Being familiar with material options (R-value, U-value, and low-E glass; see page 211) will help you weigh your options.

There are many factors to consider when purchasing windows for your home. Before you start thinking about features and upgrades for your windows, figure out what window material makes sense for your project. There are options for different climates and even for the scope of the construction.

WINDOW TYPE

The scale of your renovation will determine whether you should use replacement windows or new construction windows.

Replacement windows are designed to fit in the existing openings with no other construction required. They are installed on top of the existing interior trim. So you can just replace your windows even if you aren't renovating anything else in the house. If you have historic window casings on the interior, the windows can be installed without disturbing them. The installers will pop the old windows out and pop the new windows in. Some finishing is required outside and possibly inside. Typically it involves having aluminum capping around the windows on the outside. The disadvantages are that the window will be slightly smaller to fit in the existing opening and there isn't as much insulating ability since you're not opening things up more. But if you don't want to remove the interior trim because your scope isn't that big, you can still change the windows.

New construction windows are designed to be installed in a newly created opening or one that has had significant demo in order to install it directly to the studs or masonry. In this type of installation, any interior trim would need to be removed. The advantages are that you can have a slightly larger window, there is more access to do additional insulating, and you can install in the opening so that exterior capping is not necessary. The disadvantage is that the scope of the project is much larger.

New windows can enhance the exterior and interior of your home, like in this sunny bathroom.

WINDOW OPERATION

The next thing to think about is how you want your windows to operate. The most common way for a window to operate is double-hung.

1. Double-hung windows: Double-hung windows have an upper and a lower sash. The window sashes slide vertically up and down. With double-hung windows, both sashes are operable. Most of the time, the upper sash remains in place while the lower sash slides up and down. However, the upper sash can slide up and down as well—hence the name! Double-hung windows provide the most amount of ventilation and options, since you might want to open just the upper sash a bit while leaving the lower closed or vice versa.

2. Single-hung windows: Single-hung windows are very similar to double-hung windows except only the lower sash is operable, while the upper sash will be stationary. There isn't much benefit to having single-hung windows instead of double-hung, except perhaps that single-hung are a tiny bit cheaper.

3. Casement windows: Casement windows are a single sash that is hinged on one side. The sash will swing horizontally like a door, and a crank on the interior turns to push the window open and turning the opposite direction will close it. An interior latch must be engaged to fully secure the window shut. Casement windows will look more modern and streamlined, since they are one single sash, but they don't typically open as much as a double-hung window, because the manufacturer typically limits how far out they can swing. There are also more mechanisms, so they are slightly more prone to mechanical issues.

4. Fixed windows: As you might have guessed, a fixed window is not openable. It's just a fixed pane of glass. Since the point of windows is usually to let light and air in, this type is rare but has its purposes as well. For example, if you have an entire wall of windows, you may need only some of them to open and others may be fixed.

WINDOW MATERIAL

For each type of window material, there are factors to consider, including cost, energy efficiency, and design flexibility, to best fit the needs of your home and meet climate considerations.

WOOD WINDOWS

Wood has been used for centuries to build windows. It's a strong and attractive material and can be used to showcase different architectural styles, blend into the natural color scheme of your home, and make a beautiful first impression. If you're all about the details, wood windows may be the perfect material for you. Wood is our favorite material for windows, since we love classic wood-trim interiors and original architectural detail. With proper maintenance, wood windows can give your home a timeless and elegant look, but you should know that some maintenance is required. You'll want to inspect the exterior occasionally, remove surface dirt, touch up damaged areas, and repaint them periodically. Besides beauty, wood window frames offer several benefits, including energy efficiency. Wood insulates well and thoroughly protects interior spaces from both cold and warm weather, which can lower your heating and cooling costs throughout the year.

Window Efficiency Terms

Okay, now that we've gone over the types of windows, let's talk about some of the common materials used to make them. As you look at different options, you'll encounter some terms you'll want to understand:

R-value: R-value measures the ability of your window to prevent heat transfer, keeping the inside of your home comfortable. A higher R-value means that your window performs better at keeping heat in during the winter and keeping heat out in the summer.

U-value: U-value, or U-factor, measures how the window insulates—the lower the U-value, the better the window insulates. In regions with more dramatic seasonal temperature fluctuations, like the northern United States, keeping in heat is important. In the South, however, homeowners want to keep the heat out so the inside of their home remains a comfortable temperature.

Low-E Glass: This type of glass, also known as low-emissivity glass, has a special coating that minimizes the amount of ultraviolet rays (i.e., heat) that enters your home.

WOOD-CLAD ALUMINUM WINDOWS

You can opt to protect your wood windows with exterior aluminum cladding. Wood-clad windows (as they are known) are the best of both worlds. You can have the beauty of wood on the interior with the durability and low-maintenance of aluminum on the exterior. Window cladding can help prevent water, wind, and other weather events from damaging the integrity of your wood windows. Adding cladding to your wood windows also can help make them more energy efficient, which can reduce your utility costs. There is almost no maintenance since the aluminum protects the exterior from the elements. We use aluminum-clad wood windows often because they are less expensive than wood windows and have lower maintenance.

VINYL WINDOWS

Vinyl windows are the most affordable of the options mentioned here. Although they are a good economical option, vinyl windows also come with their share of other benefits. They are a decent insulator but usually not as good as wood. They are very low maintenance and never need painting or scraping. They can withstand harmful elements and remain functional through the years; you only have to clean them with soap and water to preserve their beauty. But they are prone to warping in sunny climates. They come in an array of colors and finishes, including ones that mimic the appearance of other materials like wood, although they are most commonly white or tan because darker colors can fade. (Other colors are available, but they come at a premium.) Overall, vinyl windows give you a great bang for your buck.

Vinyl windows have gotten a bit of a bad rap from people who think they look cheap. Although newer technology has done a better job, if design is a high priority and you have the budget for other types of windows, you shouldn't go for vinyl.

FIBERGLASS WINDOWS

Fiberglass is the strongest window material, as compared to vinyl and wood. These frames can withstand any extreme conditions. Fiberglass is also a good insulator, slightly better than vinyl, especially when more advanced construction techniques or additional insulation is added. Fiberglass is many times stronger than vinyl and resists expanding and contracting in any climate, so you get a tight, snug fit that will last. They won't stick, swell, or warp, so they will continue to open and close with ease. From a design perspective, fiberglass can be a great choice. The colors don't fade and they can be made to look almost exactly like wood. And since fiberglass is so much stronger than vinyl, the frames can be narrower. On the downside, they can be more expensive than other window types.

This steel and glass door has a thin, delicate frame that's modern and elegant, while the arched top suggests a more traditional shape.

Pros and Cons of Different Window Materials

WOOD

- Beautiful
- Great insulator
- Requires maintenance

VINYL

- Low cost
- Decent insulator
- Can warp
- Dark colors fade

FIBERGLASS

- Very durable
- Wide range of colors and styles
- Can be made to imitate wood
- Low maintenance

WINDOW FINISHES AND COLORS

There is a wide range of color and finish options for windows. White and black are very popular. If you choose wood windows, you have the option to paint or stain the interior of your windows. With wood windows you also have the option of aluminum-clad exterior in the finish. Fiberglass and vinyl can even be made to look like wood, and some of them do a pretty good job of it. Dual-color options are also available, meaning your windows can have different colors on the interior and exterior. We tend to stick with either white or black on the exterior and white, black, or stained wood on the interior. In fact, the most common windows that we install are wood-clad aluminum with black-stained interior and black exterior.

GRILLES

Grilles are another way to add character to your home's windows. If you want a traditional look, go with a smaller grille pattern with two vertical grilles (creating three panes of glass across one row). For a more modern feel, try just one vertical grille (creating two panes). We tend to do the latter even in a traditional home to modernize it a bit. You can also choose how the grille is built. Our go-to is to have the grilles in between the glass, so that you have the character of grilles, but cleaning is easier since the glass is one flat pane. You can also have the grilles on the outside of the glass, but keep in mind that you'll be cleaning multiple panels of glass separated by the grilles. Our favorite windows are wood-clad aluminum black interior and exterior with one vertical grille and one horizontal grille.

HARDWARE CHOICES

Choosing your window hardware (the latch that locks it and the handle that opens it) is important to the overall look. We tend to keep it simple and match the color to the window. When all else fails, go with black hardware!

SCREENS

Screens can be convenient, allowing you to open your windows without letting in every flying insect that comes near your house. We use them in some windows, but we avoid them in strategic areas, like the very front-facing windows, because they tend to distract from the design aesthetic of the windows.

Bifold and Sliding Doors

Your vision of your dream home might include a huge openable wall of glass. This can be a dramatic look when closed and create a relaxing indoor/outdoor lifestyle when open. There are several types of these kinds of doors:

1. Sliding Doors: A slider is usually the most economical and least complicated option. Sliding doors have a minimum of one fixed panel and one sliding panel. There can also be multiple fixed panels and up to two sliding panels that close into one another. When we have a client who wants the look of a huge wall of glass but without a huge budget, this is what we recommend. Depending on where you live, weather and insects make it less functional than your grand vision.

2. Bifold Doors: If you do want that entire wall of glass to feel open, a bifold door might be the best option. Usually they have one panel on either side that swings open like a regular door when you need to go in and out, and then at least two panels slide and fold in on one another to stack on the opposite side. If you have a bigger opening for windows, you can have more panels that bifold and stack. This type of door can be considerably more expensive and more complicated than a slider. Some manufacturers even insist that their team install it so it will work properly, which can add expense as well as concern on future maintenance.

3. Multi-Slide Doors: These doors are usually the most expensive and most complicated. Unlike bifold doors, the panels of glass slide on top of one another to one side. Since all of the panes need to slide and stack, the track needs to be much deeper than the other options.

Budget Breakdown

Facade work can be expensive, but there are some inexpensive fixes that can go a long way. Even if you do nothing else, updating your windows can have a dramatic effect. Sure, that can be expensive, too, but consider that there are some nice vinyl windows on the market now that are well priced and energy-efficient, and they look great.

Another thing that can have a huge impact but doesn't break the bank is a coat of paint. Paint the facade, paint the front door, paint the trim, paint it all, and go bold.

Finally, don't underestimate how much thinning out your landscaping and adding some new plantings can give your home's curb appeal a huge refresh.

The windows in this apartment flood the space with light and don't interrupt the view with multiple panes.

Recipe for Renovating and Updating the Exterior of Your Home

1. Stand back from the front of your home and assess its appearance. Is it off-balance or disproportionate? Does the front door stand out? Is the landscaping overgrown?

2. Update your front door by making it pop. Choose a color or finish that starts the story about what's inside.

3. Update your door hardware with something clean-lined and modern.

4. Choose house numbers in a modern and clean font that is easy to read from the street.

5. Clean up or paint the exterior.

6. Make sure your home has a well-lit front porch or entrance and add other exterior lighting, such as house number lights, up/down lights on the facade, landscaping lights, and path lighting.

7. Make sure your home's landscaping isn't hiding your house or making it look desolate. Choose flowering plants and shrubs in a limited number of colors and arrange them in repeating groupings.

8. Choose new window material, colors, and design options.

9. Be mindful of the climate where you live to understand what window options are best for you.

What You'll Need

- New front door
- New front door hardware
- House numbers in a modern font
- Front door/porch lighting
- Facade up/down lights
- Landscaping/path lighting
- Flowering plants in two or three colors
- Greenery in no more than two shades of green
- New windows in the material and finish of your choice

12

Laundry Love

Just because doing
laundry is dull doesn't
mean your laundry
room has to be!
Liven up the space
with an unexpected
choice like these bold
patterned tiles.

There are many areas in your home where function and form are very much related to one another. Feeling good in a space has as much to do with the functionality as it does to the features related to the task at hand. The room that most strongly brings this to mind is the laundry room. Let's face it, doing laundry is a task that most don't enjoy, but if your laundry area is a space you enjoy being in, it might make that dreaded job a more enjoyable experience. After all, the title of the chapter isn't Building a Laundry Room, it's Laundry Love! We are big believers in very beautiful and functional laundry areas.

When space is at a premium, compact stacked units can be a great space saver. These units are contained within a wall of storage cabinets so that they blend in seamlessly with the design.

DOES SIZE MATTER?

If you have the space for your laundry machines to have a room of their own, lucky you! But if you only have enough space to have your laundry machines in a closet, you can still make it an attractive and functional space. Before you start looking at the type of machines, here are some things to consider that will help you choose a machine that works with the space you have.

UNDERSTAND HOW MUCH SPACE YOU NEED BEHIND AND AROUND THE UNITS

Washers and dryers have connections behind them, so you'll want to make sure you account for that. These could be a water line (for washing machines), drainage, a venting duct (for dryers), and/or a gas line. The venting duct is the largest of these at about 4 inches in diameter. While some units do a better job of accounting for that extra space in their design, usually you'll want to make sure you have at least 4 inches of space behind the units. (There are exceptions we'll discuss.) With professional help and a separately sold kit, dryers can often be adapted to vent from the side if there are space limitations.

Don't forget about the doors. Front-load washers and dryers usually have a door that protrudes from the front of the unit. If you're putting the units in millwork or a closet, you'll want to account for that extra space to make sure you can close the door that the units will sit behind.

GAS OR ELECTRIC

Most washing machines run on a standard 120 V (volt) electrical outlet. Dryers come in gas or electric versions (there are two options for electrical voltage requirements). If you're not doing an extensive renovation of your home and already have one or the other, it's probably best to stick with it. If you are doing a major renovation, you may have the option to choose.

A gas dryer needs a gas line run to the location where it will be. As with all gas appliances, it also requires external venting in the form of a 4-inch duct that needs to be run outside the home. The maximum length of the duct is typically about 25 feet, though you'll want to check your local building code.

An electric dryer requires either a regular 120 V household outlet or a high-voltage 240 V outlet. Large appliances like HVAC units, induction cooktops, and electric ovens run on 240 V; if there is not currently a 240 V outlet you will need to have one run from the home's main service panel. If you don't have 240 V service available, make sure you choose a 120 V or gas unit.

A small space like a laundry room is a great place to bring in bold colors and patterns that might be overwhelming covering an entire large room.

VENTED OR VENTLESS

All gas dryers need to be vented, but electric dryers can be vented or ventless. A ventless dryer can be convenient when you don't have the ability to vent externally. Vented dryers pull moist heated air inside the unit and pull moist heated air that is expelled through the duct and outside the home. Ventless dryers work by pulling in cool, dry air from the room. The air is heated and passes through the clothes to dry them and then the warm air, which now contains moisture from the wet clothes, is cooled by causing the moisture in the air to condense and flow into a containment chamber within the dryer. As the air is dried, it is reheated and passed through the clothes again. This process continues until the clothes are dry. The containment chamber can empty either into the same drain as your washer or it can be easily emptied after each use (similarly to the way you need to clean the lint filter after each use). Usually it takes a bit longer for a ventless dryer to dry clothes than a vented dryer.

FRONT-LOAD WASHERS VS. TOP-LOAD WASHERS

We generally recommend front-load washers. Top-load washers are considered entry level, and while there are some options on the market that might fit into your beautifully renovated laundry room, front-load is usually a more modern design, and will likely give you an enjoyable laundry experience. Also, if you plan to stack your units (more on that in a bit), you will need a front-load washer. All dryers are front loading.

PEDESTALS

Washer and dryer pedestals bring your laundry appliances to a more convenient height, reducing the amount of bending needing to load and unload a unit. As an added perk, many 15-inch laundry pedestals also provide additional storage for your laundering essentials. They can give a spacious laundry room an extra-luxurious feel.

While a pedestal should not add width or depth to a washer or dryer, it will add considerable height. On average, a pedestal measures between 10 inches and 15 inches; when measuring your home's space, make sure to account for any overhead cabinetry or countertop space that may impede the installation of a pedestal.

Remember to keep practical needs in mind too; in this laundry room there's a counter for folding with open shelves above for storage.

FOLLOWING SPREAD: Why not go wild in your laundry room? Turning it into a fun space that's designed around you might just make laundry something you look forward to!

STACKED LAUNDRY UNITS

Stacking your front-load laundry units on top of one another is a great way to maximize horizontal space, provided you have the height. As with adding a pedestal, you need to account for any overhead cabinetry. You can buy a stacking kit along with your units to do this. The stacking kit ensures that the units stay locked together and don't move around while in use.

COMPACT OR FULL SIZE

Washers and dryers mainly come in two sizes: compact units and full size. (There are also some larger, high-capacity units that are used in commercial settings.)

Compact washers and dryers are 24 inches wide. They are typically about 34 inches high and 24 inches deep. They will hold roughly two baskets of laundry. The dryers are almost always electric, so you won't find many (if any) gas versions. Most run on 120 V, though a few require 240 V. They also come in ventless or vented dryer options. These models are great options if you cannot fit in full-size units.

Full-size washers and dryers are typically 27 inches wide (some are now 29 inches wide). They are usually about 39 inches high and 31 to 34 inches deep. They will hold about three baskets of laundry. The dryers can be gas (always vented) or electric (vented or ventless versions). They usually require 240 V, but there are 120 V versions.

Laundry Room Design

Once you understand the possibilities and limitations of your laundry space, it's time to consider the design! This is where you want to think as much about aesthetics as about functionality to bring a little joy into your laundry experience.

1. Storage: To make your laundry room work for you, make sure you have a place to store detergent, fabric softener, dryer sheets, wool dryer balls, and whatever else you need. We like to add some open storage shelves and some closed cabinets if there is space. It can be inexpensive to get a couple of cabinets and a small countertop.

2. Sink: If you have the ability to add plumbing for a sink, it can be very useful. A nice deep utility sink can add a design element as well as a very functional feature for stains and items that need to be hand-washed.

3. Folding, Hanging, and Drying: One of the things that might be making your laundry experience difficult is not having a dedicated space for folding clothes. If you are working with a laundry closet, think about adding either a folding table or counter or one that's mounted to the wall and can fold up when not in use.

     Be sure to include a rod or retractable hanging wire for clothes that need to air-dry.

4. Shelves, Hooks, and Baskets: Making sure everything has its place is important for your laundry room to function well and not feel cluttered. Open shelves add character to your space and give you more storage. For an added touch and to conceal anything that isn't upping the design (i.e., a bright orange detergent container), use some attractive baskets to organize your shelves. Add some hooks to provide even more opportunity for organization and add a nice touch to the space.

5. Aesthetics: Even if you want to go subtle in the kitchen and other areas of the home, the laundry room might be a place to splurge on color and pattern. Whatever you do, keep in mind that the more you make it a space you want to be in, the easier it will be to love doing your laundry!

Here are some things to think about when deciding on the look of your laundry room:

1. Wall Paneling: Wall paneling is an inexpensive feature that can bring a lot of character to your laundry room. We like to take it about two-thirds up the wall, cap it with a 1 × 2, and add some hooks. Voilà—a quaint laundry room with a ton of character that you'll enjoy being in.

2. Interesting, Fun Tile: There are so many options for a creative tile in your laundry room. It's a space where you can feel a little freer to relax and have some fun. Do something unexpected and make it a space you even want to show off!

3. Vibrant Wallpaper or Color: Adding color or vibrant wallpaper is an easy way to make your laundry room more exciting. Find something that makes you happy, and maybe doing laundry won't make you feel sad.

4. Lighting: We've talked about how lighting can create a mood and help you feel more at ease in any room, so why not give it the same attention in the laundry room. You don't need much, and you don't need to spend a lot of money. We recommend a single ceiling fixture or pendant and perhaps a couple of wall sconces if you have the space.

Budget Breakdown

The obvious place to start when you're specifying items for your laundry room is with the units themselves. Find your local appliance supplier and check their website for any upcoming sales. Appliance companies align their sales with the holiday calendar (New Year's, Presidents' Day, Fourth of July, Memorial Day, Labor Day, etc.), so there is almost always one coming up. You can also save by buying your units as a combo rather than individually. Finally, if last year's models are still available at a lower price, we seriously doubt you'll miss any major upgrades in laundry machines since the previous year.

We never put expensive cabinets or countertop material in a laundry room. Even if you're going custom in the kitchen, your laundry room is a more utilitarian space, so off-the-shelf cabinets can work just fine; we have done a lot of IKEA cabinets in laundry rooms. You also likely won't need a full slab of countertop material, so going with a stock option that is sold by the square foot can save you from buying material you don't need. Or if you're buying slabs for other areas like kitchens and bathrooms, check to see if you might have enough left over to use in the laundry room. There are very inexpensive tiles that look great in laundry rooms as well. Finding something in stock and under $8 per square feet is what we usually do.

Design features that add a lot of character and functionality, like wall hooks, shelves, and organizers, are inexpensive as well.

Recipe for Designing a Laundry Room

1. Understand that your laundry room shouldn't be purely functional. A space that's enjoyable to be in will help you get the task done.

2. Figure out what size washer and dryer you need.

3. Understand what fuel type (gas or electric) you want your dryer to be.

4. Choose whether or not your dryer needs to be vented.

5. Understand the clearance you need behind and on all sides of your units.

6. Add storage—shelves, cabinets, baskets, hooks!

7. Have a dedicated space for folding and hanging.

8. Choose some design elements that will make your space a place you want to be.

What You'll Need

- A washer and a dryer
- Gas and/or electrical, water, and waste connections
- Shelves, baskets, hooks
- Cabinets and cabinet hardware
- A sink and faucet (if you decide to install one)
- Tile
- Wall paneling or other design elements
- Wallpaper and/or paint

PART III

The Finishing Touches

It's the little things that make a room feel complete—we installed these small but mighty wall sconces on either side of this antique fireplace.

13

Your Unique Home

This room feels full
of life without feeling
overfilled, thanks to
the modern curves
and clean shapes
of the furniture and
custom built-in.

As you design each space in your home, you will have countless opportunities to add touches to make it truly unique. Those little touches are what will make you happy in your home every day and what people will swoon over when they see it. While there are plenty of things in this category that can add a lot to the budget, there are also plenty that do not. We never pass up any opportunity to add some additional architectural detail, character, and interest—especially when it doesn't add much or any cost. Are you so curious you can't stand it anymore?! Okay, let's talk about it. There are a lot of ways you can do this, but we have narrowed it down to some of our favorites. They are relatively simple things you can do yourself if you're handy. If not, you can have your architect or designer add them to your plans or just talk to your contractor about it.

Originally, this kitchen entryway featured a plain, low ceiling, making the space feel dark and crowded. By introducing an arch, we opened up the space and added architectural detail.

Nooks and Niches

One of our favorite ways to add architectural detail is through strategically placed nooks and niches. They are a simple recessed area in a wall to display artwork or have some open shelving. They can turn a boring flat wall into an interesting feature. And some of our favorite *places* to add them are in living areas, hallways, and stairways. The great thing is, if you're already building a wall, it doesn't cost much extra—if anything at all—to add this kind of detail.

Curves and Arches

Arches are timeless. They have added architectural detail for centuries (millennia maybe, who's counting). Every project we get our hands on is going to get some kind of arch. Choose one doorframe you want to feature and arch it. Or make it a theme and arch all of the doors in a room. Instead of creating a square niche in a wall, arch the top of it. Almost any hard corner in your home can be cut with a curve instead—the edge of a counter, a kitchen island, or bathroom vanity. After all, you don't want everything in your home to be the same color, so why would you want all the angles to be 90 degrees?

Wall Moulding and Paneling

We love the vintage and classic detail that wall or picture-frame moulding brings to a space. So we use it to add sophistication in a historic home and character in a new condo. It works well in living areas, dining rooms, and bedrooms. It's even a neutral enough feature to put everywhere; you can go big and use it throughout an entire room or you can go small and make it a feature. One of the best parts is that it's a relatively inexpensive and doable DIY project for anyone; see chapter 9 for more how-to detail.

Wall paneling is also a great way to add character and thoughtful detail. It's perfect for a coat nook or mudroom, laundry room, or even a bathroom. We like to bring it up to different heights depending on the room. In a mudroom, it might go three-quarters of the way up the wall, with some hooks for hanging coats. In the bathroom, we would bring it up between 40 and 48 inches, the same way you might put tile on a lower half of the wall.

A custom niche at the top of a staircase is the perfect place to feature art and other items. Unlike a bookcase, a niche creates display space without a footprint.

Lighting (Natural and Installed)

Lighting can transform a space dramatically. The name of the game is really the more, the better. Unless you're building a movie theater or photography studio, you probably aren't trying to limit the amount of light in a space.

Let's start with natural light: Take every opportunity to introduce light and bounce it around. Add skylights wherever you can. Think about glass transoms over interior doors. Make windows bigger. Get exterior doors with glass in them.

You can also set the mood with your interior lighting. Install dimmers on as many ceiling lights as you can, especially recessed lighting. Look for light fixtures made of interesting materials like ceramic, metals, wood, plaster, or fabric. Introduce a mix of hanging pendants, chandeliers, and flush and semi-flush mount lights. We love wall sconces! Use them in hallways, flank a fireplace or bed on both sides, light shelves or pictures, and add ambient light. Mix in floor and table lamps to light specific areas and create cozy spaces in your rooms.

Slatting, Reeding, and Fluting

Look for opportunities to build in some textures with reeding, fluting, or slatting. Reeding creates a rounded convex pattern, fluting creates a rounded concave pattern, and slatting creates a flat groove pattern. You can buy panels of any of these or have a woodworker or plaster worker create some. It looks great in furniture, but it can also be used as cladding on a wall, the back side of a kitchen island, or a kitchen exhaust hood.

In any home, natural light is essential. It can be hard to come by in historic homes, so it pays to get creative! This elongated skylight brightens the staircase on all three floors.

Colors and Paint

This one might seem obvious, but you can use color and paint to make your home unique. Beyond just picking a nice color and painting the wall, here are some other ideas:

1. **Paint the ceiling.** Most people paint their walls and leave the ceiling white, but bringing the color up to the ceiling will create a dramatic space. Or maybe even choose a complementary or contrasting color for the ceiling.

2. **Paint the trim too.** Call us crazy, but we aren't fans of dark wall colors with white trim. The contrast is harsh, and it feels like something was forgotten. So paint the trim the same color as the walls or even a complementary color.

3. **Paint bookshelves and niches.** Remember our first recommendation in this chapter to add nooks and niches in the wall around your home (see page 238)? Well, they don't have to be the same color as the wall. Feature them more prominently by painting them a different color.

4. **Go bold!** You don't need to paint all of your walls purple, but consider picking at least one small room to go bold in! Maybe an office, dining room, or powder room. And yes, a dramatic eggplant color might be exactly what it needs!

5. **Textures.** Instead of just painting a wall, you can add texture to it with a plaster or limewash application. Tadelakt (for wet areas like backsplashes and even showers; see page 84) or limewash can add variation and interest to any wall. It looks great in a vibrant color or even if you want to keep things neutral but still add some detail. You can use these types of plaster rather than painting a wall a flat color or instead of using tile in powder rooms and bathrooms.

6. **Contrast and tones.** You can use contrast (or lack of contrast) to create a mood in your home. A living room with a neutral-on-neutral palette is going to have a sophisticated and airy feel. If you want to punch up the color, try using two tones of the same color. A light and dark blue, or a couple of shades of pink, can be an interesting contrast. Contrast can be used in small doses or entire rooms.

From the tub to the wallpaper to the wainscoting to the door, this bathroom is a bold color haven! Don't be afraid to mix different shades of the same color.

How to Limewash Walls

Limewash is a textured paint that gives your walls a beautiful, nuanced feel. You'll see variation in the color and texture, which can give the wall a chalky, suede-like look. Limewash is made from limestone that's been crushed, fired at high temperature, and mixed with water and pigments. Limewash is different from Venetian plaster, which is much thicker and tends to have a more polished and formal finish. It works well on plaster, stone, and brick. When applied to drywall, you'll want to use an acrylic primer first, although many modern premade varieties may already have the binding additives, so check the instructions with the brand you decide to use.

Limewash becomes much lighter as it dries. Typically up to three coats are applied. The first coat will be very translucent, the second will become opaquer, and the third coat (if used) provides the finished look. You have to be open to a bit of chance for the final look. Colors and texture will vary based on the technique you use, the pigment in the paint, and even what surface it's painted on.

WHAT YOU NEED:

- Limewash paint (depending on what you use, you may need to mix it)

- Acrylic primer (allows the limewash to be absorbed)

- Block brush with natural bristles

- Painter's tape and drop cloth to keep the area clean

PREPPING WALLS FOR LIMEWASH

Limewash paint can be applied directly over breathable surfaces such as brick, cement, stucco, and plaster. The most common application is on drywall, since that's what most wall surfaces will be today. Keep in mind that drywall and previously painted surfaces should be primed with an acrylic primer. Just roll it on. One coat should be enough, but follow the limewash paint company's instructions.

APPLICATION

If you weren't already having fun, this is where you will! You should use a block brush with natural bristles to apply the limewash. It's very important to use the right kind of brush. It should be thick with lots of bristles. One of the most common techniques is the cloud pattern technique. Pick a place to start on the wall that isn't too close to the edge or corner. Make a center point and create random and multidirectional strokes, working your way outward from the center. Spread the paint out as far as it naturally goes with soft edges on the "cloud." Make sure to brush in multiple directions, up, down, and crisscross. Once you spread the paint to form one cloud, move to the next. Pick a point on the wall not too close to your first cloud, but close enough so that once it's fully spread they will begin to join. Repeat the process until the wall is covered with the first coat. Note that it will be fairly translucent and won't provide complete coverage, but that's what the next coat is for! The limewash will dry much lighter. So if it seems too dark when wet, keep in mind that it will lighten considerably. Wait for it to dry fully to start the second coat. Repeat the process again with clouds, but start on the opposite side. Once you are done with the second coat, you should see more consistent coverage and the textures will begin to appear. Once it's dried fully, decide if you need a third coat.

TIP: Our favorite limewash paints are from Portola Paint, JH Wall Paints, and Bauwerk.

PAGE 245:

The limewash paint in this studio apartment brings texture and variation. Even in a smaller space, you can still go with a darker tone on the walls without making it feel confined.

Built-Ins

Putting in built-ins is a great way to add character and additional storage to a space. We think built-ins look best when they go from the floor to ceiling and wall to wall. Either side of a fireplace is a great choice, and built-ins across a blank wall will give it purpose.

Glass Interior Doors and Partitions

We're giving this one a section of its own because it has become one of the features we have used in our designs that's the most popular. It all started when we renovated our home and were designing our vintage-inspired guest bathroom. We decided to get a vintage door, cut it to size, cut out the top panel, and put in a frosted chicken wire glass in the top (see opposite and page 179). Many of our clients ask us for this as well, so we have done lots of different versions of it. (Once we did it on every interior door in the house!) It's still one of our favorite projects to take on and it always adds character. Give it a go!

Opaque glass doors create privacy without shrinking a space or sacrificing valuable natural light. They allow rooms to feel both intimate and airy at the same time.

Architectural Items

Some of the houses that we work in already have beautiful architectural details, and some don't, either because they were very unfortunately removed (who would do that, right?!) or it is a newer building that never had them. In either case, we know ways to add them or add them back. This usually involves finding items from architectural salvage. There are lots of opportunities to add architectural items. Take a look at a local salvage store and see if anything calls out to you. We've gotten everything from sinks, tubs, lights, exterior corbels, ceiling medallions, pier mirrors, and more.

One architectural feature we add most often is a fireplace. Sure, it would be great to add a working fireplace, but if that isn't possible, why not add a salvaged fireplace facade to inject massive amounts of character to your home? We've put them into homes in the exact spot one might have been removed from, and we have put them into new condo apartments where they never existed. Either way, once they're installed they look like they have always been there.

Vintage Items

Adding vintage items throughout your home is one of the best ways to make it feel special. Vintage items are usually one of a kind, and the long life they have had gives your space depth. Trust us, when guests ask you about it, you'll happily tell them the story of how and where you found it. Some of our favorite vintage items to find and use are art, lamps, furniture pieces (we usually go for the smaller pieces like coffee tables, side tables, and chairs), rugs, dressers, and armoires.

Budget Breakdown

Making your home unique might be something that you find addictive. Once you add that first special feature that you are in love with, every day you're going to want more and more. Many of these ideas are very easy to DIY, which gives you an even greater appreciation for each one, and you'll beam with pride when someone compliments you on it. Doing a limewash application on your walls, installing some floating shelves, maybe even doing a little drywall work to create a wall niche are all totally doable projects! We included a few how-to sections here in this book, but trust us when we tell you that you can learn almost anything from watching YouTube videos or reading a blog. Pick a project, get started, and see if you found your new passion.

Our basement workspace doesn't get any natural light, so we had to be very intentional about installing light sources. The backlit stained glass panel gives the illusion of natural light!

Recipe for Making Your Home Unique

1. As you design each space, look for opportunities to add unique touches.

2. Look for inspiration from other spaces that you love for features you can build into your home.

3. Remember that many of these features are not expensive but make your space very special.

4. Don't be afraid to do something bold. If you love it in an inspiration photo, chances are you'll love it in your home too.

What You'll Need

- Inspiration for unique features to do in your home
- Supplier for a DIY project or a professional to do it for you
- Confidence!

14
Historic Home Love

You never know what's hiding underneath layers of paint and varnish in a historic home! This newel post was covered in white paint and took skill and time to uncover completely.

R enovating a historic home comes with unique challenges and rewards. The sense of accomplishment we have when we fully restore a home's original features just doesn't compare to anything else that we do. The best part about a historic home is all of the charming original features it comes with. One of our favorite things about renovating is working with the amazing artisans in their respective fields—wood restorers, plaster artists, stained glass specialists, stone workers, and many more—to revive and restore these unique elements, which is what we'll cover in this chapter.

A historic home renovation can take a lot of patience and skill. So it's important to bring in the right professionals for the job. Some general contractors may have skills or subcontractors for some of these areas, but we usually find that we need to bring in specialists. Wood restoration, plaster restoration, stained glass work, and facade work are all areas that take special care to fully restore. While the professionals will be doing a lot of the work, it's important to know what can be done and how they will do it.

Tall, double entry doors are signature features of brownstones. If you're renovating a historic home, take the time to research the architectural elements unique to that style of residence.

Wood Restoration

The beautiful original woodwork in historic homes is really hard to replicate, as it was usually carved by hand. In some of the houses that we work in, we find it painted over with many layers of globby paint. A bad paint job on top of a previous bad paint job is not a good combination! One of our favorite things to do to transform a historic home is to strip the woodwork back to its original beauty. Seeing those many layers of paint come off is so rewarding. It's like a walk back through time as each layer is removed.

Stripping wood is a tough job. We rely on professionals who have a lot of experience. Unfortunately, it involves chemicals that can be dangerous and techniques that can damage the wood if you don't know what you're doing. If it's a smaller job or if you just want to give it a go, there are a lot of DIY products out there. We have found the most successful way is using a heat gun to remove the majority of the paint, then using a chemical stripper to remove what doesn't come up with the heat gun. After that, the wood is cleaned with denatured alcohol and steel wool. By now you should be able to see the beautiful wood in all its glory. Continue to clean with the denatured alcohol until it's completely freed from its paint prison! Once it is stripped completely raw, we like to put on something to finish and condition it. If you do want to stain it, now would be the time, but we prefer just putting on something like tung oil or a clear matte water-based polyurethane.

Floor Restoration

One common problem with old houses is crooked floors! Years of settling and sagging of the joists can cause it. It's one of the things we look for when we first see a new project that's an old house. If the floors have severe grades, we know it's going to be a big job. Although underlying structural issues can be the problem, if a bearing wall below wasn't removed or some other structural alteration done, it's usually just a cosmetic issue. Unfortunately, it usually means the floors have to come up to fix the issue. Sometimes the original floors can be salvaged but often they'll have to be fixed. The fix involves removing all of the flooring and subfloor until the saggy joists are exposed and then attaching a new piece of lumber onto the old joist (also called "sistering") to bring it back up to a level surface. Since the floor sagging is what is causing the slanted floors, sistering brings it up to the highest point. Then a new subfloor can be laid and a new floor on top of it. If that sounds like a big job, it is, but unfortunately that's not all of that. There are often other adjustments that need to be made as a result. As the floor comes up to its

This antique door required meticulous care to remove the old paint. The restored piece now stands as a testament to the home's timeless elegance.

new level surface, you'll need to adjust the doors, trim like baseboards and door casings, as well as the stairs, as heights may change.

If you are lucky and have original floors that are relatively level, you can likely just restore them. A flooring expert who specializes in historic floor restoration is best. They can fill in damaged and missing pieces, sand everything down, and refinish it. One of the biggest questions is if there is enough wood left for the floors to be sanded and refinished. Since historic floors are made from solid wood, that's usually not a problem. Our finish of choice is a clear matte polyurethane like Bona Traffic HD in extra matte.

Plaster Restoration

Plaster work can be the star of the show in a historic home. When you walk into an old house and you're struck by its charm, it might be the plaster crown mouldings and medallions that are doing it for you. Most modern crown moulding just doesn't replicate the look of plaster. We go out of our way to save it, often making it a priority over other things. One problem is that it can be a bit delicate, and water damage and other issues can make it crack. That's when we know we need one of the skilled plaster artisans we work with to come in and help! Watching them do their work is one of our favorite things—but keep in mind that it is not inexpensive work. There are few people who do it, and those who do are more artists than tradespeople, so that skilled work comes with a cost. We think it's worth it!

If you do have plaster crown moulding and you need to repair a section, the only way to do that is to have a skilled plaster worker spend many hours re-creating the moulding. If you need to replace it all, you can buy new plaster moulding that is precast. Then it can be put up with much less effort on-site. It's also possible to get new mouldings made of other materials, but if you want that historical plaster look, our advice is to avoid wood. There are lots of nice wood profiles for crown moulding out there (see page 180), but we don't think any of them do a good job giving you that beautiful plaster crown moulding look. The reason is that you don't get a deep enough cove (the rounded concave part of crown moulding) with wood. The material just doesn't work that way. There are options made from plaster-covered foam, polyurethane, and other synthetic materials that do a great job of replicating plaster, are much less expensive than plaster, and look beautiful once installed.

We took this wainscoting from globby mess to crisp and clean. Set against the deep black staircase, the pristine white wainscoting brings an elegance to the space.

Staircases

We have an affinity for original staircases. The banister, balusters, and posts remind us of all the people who have gone up and down, living their lives, over the centuries. We don't mind a little squeak and will opt to keep what we have and repair it rather than replace it whenever we can.

Let's start with the **banister**. We've stripped paint from many balusters, railings, and newel posts, and we are always happy with what we see. You can rarely buy new balusters off the shelf to match, and that's one of the things we love about them. When we have damaged or missing ones, we have them made at a local wood shop. We just take one over and the woodworkers spin as many new ones as we need using the same species of wood. Sometimes we have an additional handrail made as well. It can get a little tricky with curves, turns, and details you might find on a newel post. For that, we bring in a skilled woodworker who can replicate what we need. We know that might all sound expensive, but it's likely less so than replacing everything.

Now for the **treads and risers**. You may have the same problem here as with some of your original floors: Often the original stairs sag and end up leaning to the side, making you feel like you're in a fun house. Depending on how severe the lean is, we sometimes cough it up to a bit of character, but if it's something that bothers you, it can be fixed. It usually involves removing the banister (so it can be replaced later). We've jacked up staircases and built in a new structure, and we have also leveled each stair individually and replaced the treads. A professional will be able to help you determine what can be done.

If they are in really bad shape, however, you may want to replace them. The treads can be sanded and the risers can be stripped and refinished, but as you can imagine, stairs often take a beating over the years. This is another place where we don't mind a bit of character.

If you want to save your original stairs but they are very squeaky, that can also be fixed to some degree. It may be possible to repair them from underneath. There is often plaster on the underside of the stairs that can be removed so that the structural workings are exposed. Screws, new pieces of wood, and glue can be used to stabilize what is moving around and causing the squeaks. After the repairs are made, the plaster can be repaired or drywall can be installed to look just the way it always did.

Staircases can be absolute art pieces, but they also need to be incredibly functional. Here, we improved the quality of the steps to make them safe and durable, while restoring the banister.

Doors, Trim, and Moulding

Restoring your original doors, trim, and moulding often goes hand in hand with wood stripping and restoration. We love saving old doors. They often have beautiful details. If they are painted, they can be stripped. If they are damaged, a woodworker can replace parts and pieces of them. If you have some original doors but need new ones for additional locations, you can have a woodworker remake them exactly. You can do the same thing with original baseboards and casings. It's a bit more expensive, but you might find that it doesn't cost that much more than buying new off-the-shelf doors, trim, and mouldings. Since some of it will already be installed, you only need to get the additional amount that you need.

Hardware and Hinges

Those beautiful original doors might also have some amazing original hardware. You can make them like new again; all you need is a Crock-Pot! We use just water, a bit of liquid detergent, and a long soak in a Crock-Pot set on Low. You can also use chemicals, but there is usually no need with the Crock-Pot method.

Fireplaces and Flues

If you're lucky enough to have a home with a beautiful original fireplace, we are jealous! It's one of the features that just screams "charm" in an old home. If your fireplace isn't in great shape or isn't functional, getting it back in working order might be high on your list of priorities. Some fireplace facades are just for show, and you might be okay with the charm they bring even if you can't light a fire. We see a lot of marble fireplace facades and mantels that have been painted. We always wonder why anyone would do that! Fortunately, you can strip off the paint to reveal the beautiful stone. We like to use a peel-away stripper. After the stripper is applied, it's covered in special laminated paper sheets and left on for days until it is peeled off, taking all the paint off with it. It works great on marble. The stone can then be cleaned with acetone to remove stains and discoloring.

If you have a wood fireplace facade, you may also want to strip off the paint or varnish. It works the same as stripping any other wood in your home. Wood fireplace facades often have tile or stone around the opening in the center, which can be in really bad shape. Also, and we are not afraid to say this, some of the colors or styles originally chosen (or perhaps replaced early in its life) just aren't, well, very attractive. So if the tile is in bad shape and not that cute, we don't mind changing it. We get to keep the beautiful original facade and mantel but breathe some new life into it by updating this feature.

If you do plan to use your fireplace for burning wood, you'll want to make sure the flue is clean and operating properly. A professional should inspect it to be sure. The flue can be relined if needed so that it works again. Brickwork can even be done to repair the firebox or chimney.

Stained Glass

While this stained glass isn't original to our home, it certainly blends with the antique, old school vibes of our basement workspace.

If you are fortunate enough to have original stained glass in your home, it is certainly worth saving and repairing. This is another opportunity for you to work with a wonderful artisan who practices a dying art. One of our favorite places to visit is our local stained glass artist's workshop. We could spend hours listening as he tells us about all the amazing houses he has worked in, looking at different colors of beautiful glass, and hearing about the Brooklyn of old.

Exterior Facade

A historic home's facade can be one of the most charming parts of the house. It's also one of the things that protects your home and keeps the elements out. Old stone can crumble and wood can rot if not protected. We do a lot of work in Brooklyn brownstones, which are made of a unique material. It was originally mined locally in the northeastern United States, and it was used specifically because it's soft and moldable. It could be carved into ornate shapes above the doors and windows, sometimes with faces of animals or people. The problem is that this soft material doesn't last forever. Other types of facade material aren't too different; wood and other types of stone eventually need some repair.

To replace **brownstone**, all of the existing material is chipped off. Typically there is a masonry facade under the cosmetic brownstone facade. A brownstone facade is applied in several layers. The first layer is the slurry coat, mixed thinner so it binds to the brick. The next layer is called the scratch coat. It's a stucco-concrete mix that's used to form the brownstone into its original shape. That layer needs to dry fully before the final coat of brownstone. Careful attention is paid to match the original color. When the last layer of brownstone is applied, the finer details, such as ornaments and flowers, are added. The work is done by hand, using levels, trowels, sponges, and other tools of the trade.

If you have a **brick** home, the most common maintenance is repointing. Brick is a very solid building material, but the mortar between them can decay and erode, compromising the wall. A mason can scrape out a bit of the old mortar and put in new solid mortar. You might be staring at your brick wall and thinking, *Wow! There are a lot of bricks and mortar joints. That must take a while!* You're right, it's a big job and will take some time. Once this is done the exterior walls will last for decades more and will look beautiful!

If the exterior of your home is **wood,** you will likely have maintenance to perform. If the exterior has been maintained over the years, wood can last for many decades. But if maintenance was deferred, it can cause a lot of problems. Painting is the best way to make sure the exterior wood on your home is protected. Once the paint goes, the wood will be right behind it. If there is rot, the wood will need to be replaced. For ongoing maintenance, annually scrape and sand any peeling paint, and every few years paint it all completely.

Windows

We covered most of what you need to know about replacing your windows in chapter 11. But what if you have a historic home with original windows that you want to keep but you just want them to work better? If you're dealing with drafty windows, wood rot, or broken panes, it can be fixed!

Up to 85 percent of window heat loss is through its poorly weather-sealed sashes rather than through the single-paned glass. Installing weatherstripping between the two sashes can reduce cold air coming in from outside. Weatherstripping can be applied along the edges of any window and is an inexpensive way to reduce noise and drafts from coming in.

You can also install window inserts or storm windows on the interior or exterior to stop the elements from entering when the original windows aren't cutting it. This is going to change the aesthetics a bit, so it could be something you want to avoid.

All exterior wood needs to be painted regularly to ensure that it is protected. You should inspect your wood windows for any peeling paint or rot. You can often selectively restore the wooden window where it's damaged rather than replacing the frame entirely, which is not only cost-effective but more environmentally friendly.

If you have broken windowpanes, you can replace them by having new glass panes cut to size and inserted into existing window sashes or muntins (the vertical and horizontal elements that divide a window's glass into a grid) by removing old putty or caulk, inserting the new panes, and re-puttying or caulking. Pay attention to the aesthetics of the original glass to ensure that you don't end up with a patchwork of clearly old or new individual glass panes. Old glass sometimes has small bubbles or a waviness on the surface, and sometimes there's even a greenish tint. Glass suppliers will have something that could be similar, or you can use recycled glass for an even better match.

Finally, if your original windows aren't closing and opening easily, it could be the system of weights and balances to assist with opening and closing the heavy sashes. The pulleys and ropes are located along the side of the window. The ropes can deteriorate and break, and the pulleys can get stuck. Replacing the rope and lubricating or replacing the pulleys can make them operate as good as new!

The joys of restoring original features can't be beat. If you have a house that has them, they're probably what attracted you to it in the first place! It's worth the extra time, effort, and cost in our opinion.

Budget Breakdown

The unfortunate news for your budget is that restoring an old house can be expensive, though there are ways to save. One of the most obvious can be to use what is there. If you can sand and refinish original floors, you can avoid the expensive cost of new flooring material. If you can reuse original doors, trim, and moulding, then you can save on materials there as well. You'll need to commit some budget to restoring them, but hopefully that cost will be less than purchasing new. (You'll want to be careful, though, to weigh the cost of the restoration versus getting new items; that often depends on the condition it's in and the quality of the original stuff.) In the houses that we work in, the upper floors' original trim sometimes isn't as high quality or ornate. Going through the expensive and labor-intensive process of stripping and restoring it might not be worth it, and instead we can replace it with something new that will be in keeping with the original items. We will have a better finished result and aren't sacrificing an original item that we thought was worth the effort to keep. Restoring a historic home is definitely a balancing act, and while we want to keep as much of the original home as we can, it's good to be realistic that sometimes it makes more sense simply to replace items.

Recipe for Restoring a Historic Home

1. Determine what original features your home has and what needs to be restored.

2. Keep in mind that this is a place you need a healthy budget to do right.

3. Bring in skilled professionals who know how to restore these original features, or if you feel like you can tackle it yourself, study up!

4. Remember that you may need to replace some or all of the features to really bring the house back to life. Most things can be re-created, and sometimes you can look for modern alternative materials that can accomplish what is needed.

What You'll Need

- Love and appreciation for historic home architecture

- Patience to deal with the decades-old materials

- A solid budget to restore the original features

- Skilled artisans who do this type of restoration work

15

Outdoor Living

This modern carriage
house wraps around
a unique inner
courtyard that
provides the ultimate
indoor-outdoor living
experience.

Y our home's outdoor space is important for many things. It might be where the kids play, where the dog runs, and where you get a bit of fresh air every now and then. But why not dedicate part of it—whether it's a spacious yard or cozy patio—to create an area for an outdoor living space? We decided to close the book with this chapter because we've found that many people decide to tackle their outdoor space as a phase two, after the interior work is complete and they are happily moved in. It's the ultimate finishing touch to your beautifully renovated home.

This backyard has areas for entertaining, dining, cooking, planting, and playing. It's a perfect escape from the bustle of the busy streets outside the home.

Before you start with design and furnishings, think about how the outdoor space will be used and plan accordingly. Here are some questions to ask yourself:

Do you want to host outdoor dinner parties or barbecues?

How many guests do you typically entertain?

Are you looking for a quiet space to relax and unwind?

Does your space need a separate area just for pets or kids?

Is your space tiny and you want to maximize its impact? Or is your space so large you need to break it up into smaller, purposeful areas?

The answers to these questions will help guide your design.

Layout and Design Elements

Start with what you feel is the most important use for your outdoor space. It's okay if you have multiple priorities. So if it's for dogs, kids, a vegetable garden, or even a pool . . . set aside the space and go to town! If you want a place to entertain and relax, build that in too. Consider the size of your space and work from the top priority down.

Most of what we'll talk about in this chapter is about making an enjoyable, relaxing, outdoor living space, an extension of your indoor living space. It usually makes the most sense for the outdoor living space to be next to or close to the house, but there are some reasons that might not be true, such as if you want a dining area in a secluded back part of the garden, or you want to orient it in a place to maximize a view. You will likely also want access to electricity and, if you really want to do it up, running water (hence why it usually makes sense to be close to the house). Finally, make the most of any views your property has to offer. It doesn't have to be an ocean or a mountain view. Maybe it's a glimpse of the evening sky at sunset, a peek of the first sun coming through the trees in the morning, or a view of the garden you spend so much time tending.

Now it's time to lay out the living space. Use the same thoughtfulness as if you were designing the floor plan of your home. Your outdoor room(s) should have a logical and functional connection to the inside of the house, like locating the outdoor dining area near the kitchen. The most useful outdoor rooms allow guests to easily move from the indoor entertaining areas to the outdoor. We recommend an area for sitting and relaxing with comfortable seating, an area for dining, and an area for cooking.

We used bright color to make this small outdoor space happy and inviting. The glimpses you get from inside make it as much of a part of the interior design as the outdoors.

HARDSCAPE

Before you start bringing in the furniture, you'll probably want to create some hardscaping for the living areas. Hardscaping includes all of the nonliving parts of our outdoor design, like the stone pavers, walkways, wood decks and pergolas, and fencing. You'll want to leave some area for plantings and have enough hardscape for chairs, a table, and other furniture. We like to use pavers in flagstone, bluestone, or porcelain. We are also suckers for the Mediterranean vibe (and cost savings!) of pea gravel pebbles. Be sure to include plantings and pots close to or even inside the living areas to integrate the space with the outdoors.

FURNITURE

Similar to your home's indoor entertaining spaces, you can create areas for sitting, dining, and cooking. Select furniture that's comfortable but also practical for outdoor use. The last thing you want is for your outdoor living space to look uninviting after one season. Use colors and patterns to bring your interior style outside.

SEATING

We like to have some sort of seating arrangement with an outdoor couch or chairs with cushions. A coffee table and moveable side tables can create a living room–like feel. Just as you did in your indoor living room, make it inviting for conversation. Place the seating across from or perpendicular to one another, with a coffee table in front for drinks and snacks. Anchor it all with an outdoor rug. One of the keys to making it feel cozy is paying attention to what's above. We like to have hanging lighting, plants, or umbrellas to define the space.

DINING AREA

Bring in similar elements from your indoor dining room; choose pieces that your friends and family will want to spend a long time with. Set the mood with an outdoor candelabra. For lighting, why not hang an outdoor chandelier or light fixture over the table—or even a string of lights?

This ultra comfortable and durable outdoor couch from West Elm makes this outdoor seating area feel like just another room in the home.

COOKING AREA

We are happy just having a grill outside and like to put it close to the outdoor living and dining areas so everyone can be part of the fun. If you have a bit more space, you can even build an outdoor kitchen complete with a countertop, cooktop, undercounter fridge, and sink with running water. One of our favorite new gadgets that is always a huge crowd-pleaser is the outdoor wood-fired pizza oven. Everyone can choose their own toppings and watch their food cook right in front of them.

FIRE

When evenings are cool, don't move the party inside. Extend your outdoor entertaining season by creating a firepit or fireplace area with comfortable seating. Enjoy evenings being warmed by the fire and use your outdoor area year-round in milder climates.

WATER

For a refreshing and relaxing addition to your space, consider adding a water feature. It doesn't need to be an elaborate fountain or waterfall, even a trickle can have an impact.

PLANT SELECTION

Leave lots of area in your outdoor space for plantings. You can use planters to separate or define spaces. One of the most important things to consider is how much light each area gets and how much maintenance you are able to handle. If your outdoor space is always shady, be sure to get plants that will thrive in that environment. If you have plenty of sun, then take full advantage of it. We recommend easy-care greenery in and around your outdoor living space for low maintenance. Mix in some flowering plants and develop a pattern as we talked about in chapter 11 (see page 206). An outdoor living space is the perfect area to use the vertical surface to build in a green wall. We like the look and feel of having planters and pots in our outdoor living space in addition to the plants in the ground.

Al fresco dining is one of the best ways to make your outdoor space and extension of our living space. This big table with ample seating overlooking the treetops of Brooklyn is perfect for lingering dinner parties.

LIGHTING

Make your outdoor space a true extension of your home by incorporating lighting to set the mood. Illuminate outdoor cooking areas to allow more meal prep to be done outside. Create visual interest and expand the feel of the space by uplighting trees or fencing farther out in the yard. Add decorative lighting to brighten steps and pathways. Path lighting adds an extra layer of illumination for you and your guests to safely move around in the outdoor spaces after dark. In addition to serving a decorative function, path lights can highlight a garden feature or tree with directional uplight. Ambient path lights feature a decorative shade that diffuses the light, adding ambience to your garden or patio.

The Finishing Touches

Adding a colorful patterned rug is the perfect way to complete any living space, so why not do it outside too? There are a lot of outdoor rugs that are as easy to hose off as the patio. Putting a rug in the space can make it feel cozier and enhance the outdoor-living-room feel. Accessories like seat cushions, placemats, hanging plants, pots, ceramics, and lights can complete the look!

Budget Breakdown

When we renovated our home, we spent everything we could to make the interior what we dreamed, and our backyard was phase two. Yards, patios, and balconies are great projects to tackle later. Even when we finally felt we had the budget to work on our backyard, it wasn't enough to do anything extravagant, but we still wanted a beautiful outdoor space. We decided to build a planter to separate a sitting area from the social area. We installed a combination of pea gravel as well as bluestone pavers we salvaged from our own backyard. We prepped and planted grass seed and added some plantings. We got a couple of inexpensive teak love seats with cushions, a firepit that has a wood cover and doubles as a cocktail table, two Adirondack chairs, and a hammock. For lighting we have two long strands of lights that span our entire backyard. Finally, we added some creative touches with painted pots and tiki torches. The result was a space where we have spent countless hours together and with friends. It's simple but beautiful, and the entire project cost us only about $5,000—tens of thousands less than the quotes we got from landscape companies.

If you don't have a big backyard budget, you can follow these same guidelines. Tackle the project yourself and use inexpensive, simple materials.

Recipe for Creating an Outdoor Living Space

1. Determine the top priorities for your outdoor space.

2. Based on the amount of space you have, work from your top priority down.

3. Choose a location for your outdoor living space, paying attention to your access to electricity, water, any views your outdoor space has, and an easy transition from the inside.

4. Once your location is decided, lay out the space. We like to have areas for living, dining, and cooking, just like in your home's interior.

5. Lay your hardscape to create a comfortable area for furniture.

6. Create an area for socializing and dining with comfortable furniture.

7. Include lots of areas for plantings.

8. Make it cozy with an outdoor rug and overhead lighting.

9. Include some personal touches and decor.

What You'll Need

- An outdoor space, large or small
- A layout for your space that includes your top priorities
- Hardscape material like pavers or pea gravel
- Plants and planters
- Furniture for sitting, such as an outdoor couch and/or chairs
- Furniture for dining, like a table and chairs
- A grill or other outdoor kitchen equipment
- Lighting
- Other decor items

Reference Illustrations

KITCHEN

CABINET DOORS

RAISED PANEL

SHAKER

FLAT PANEL

OPEN SHELVING

CABINET FRONTS

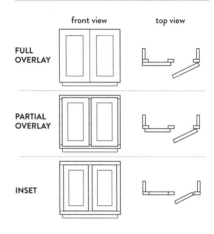

front view   top view

FULL OVERLAY

PARTIAL OVERLAY

INSET

BACKSPLASH TILE PATTERNS

VERTICAL STACKED

HORIZONTAL STACKED

RUNNING BOND

CHEVRON

BASKET WEAVE

HERRINGBONE

KITCHEN HOOD

CHIMNEY

UNDER CABINET

MICRO

CUSTOM

KITCHEN LIGHTING

PENDANT   GLOBE   RUSTIC

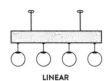

LINEAR

CHANDELIER

KITCHEN CABINET HARDWARE

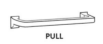

PULL

FLAT KNOB

CUP PULL

CRYSTAL KNOB

EDGE PULL

ROUND KNOB

BATHROOM

VANITY TYPES

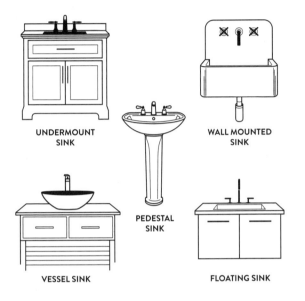

UNDERMOUNT
SINK

PEDESTAL
SINK

WALL MOUNTED
SINK

VESSEL SINK

FLOATING SINK

BATHROOM FAUCETS

COUNTER-MOUNTED
SINGLE HOLE

COUNTER-MOUNTED
3-HOLE WIDESPREAD

WALL-MOUNTED
WIDESPREAD

WALL-MOUNTED
SINGLE HANDLE

BATHROOM TILE PATTERNS

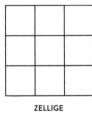

ZELLIGE

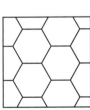

HEX

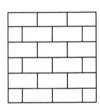

SUBWAY

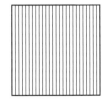

WOODLOCK

MARBLE

CEMENT

CLOSET

DOORS

CLOSET DOORS

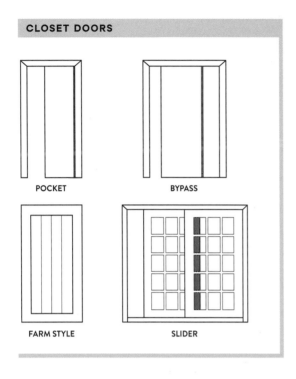

POCKET

BYPASS

FARM STYLE

SLIDER

FRONT DOOR STYLES

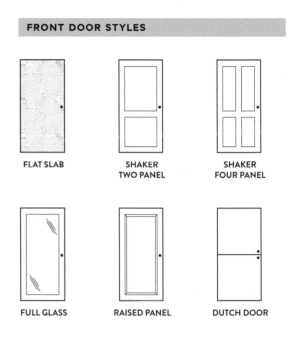

FLAT SLAB

SHAKER
TWO PANEL

SHAKER
FOUR PANEL

FULL GLASS

RAISED PANEL

DUTCH DOOR

DOORSWING

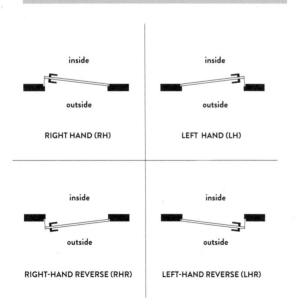

RIGHT HAND (RH)

LEFT HAND (LH)

RIGHT-HAND REVERSE (RHR)

LEFT-HAND REVERSE (LHR)

DOOR PARTS

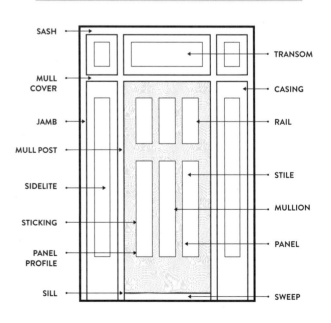

WINDOWS

HERRINGBONE

DOUBLE HERRINGBONE

CHEVRON

CHANTILLY

BASKET WEAVE

DOUBLE BASKET WEAVE

MOSAICS

VERSAILLES

WINDOW PARTS

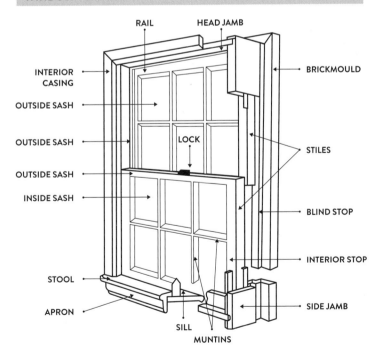

RAIL

HEAD JAMB

INTERIOR CASING

BRICKMOULD

OUTSIDE SASH

OUTSIDE SASH

LOCK

STILES

OUTSIDE SASH

INSIDE SASH

BLIND STOP

INTERIOR STOP

STOOL

APRON

SIDE JAMB

SILL

MUNTINS

Acknowledgments

JORDAN

To my mom and dad: Thank you for raising me with gentleness, love, and support. Dad, thank you for being the businessman you are; while you might not have let me run your business, I always knew that you lead with heart. Mom, you have always been my biggest supporter. I think the bulletin boards you let me create in your classroom inspired me to follow a design path. Your care for others is something I try to pay forward each and every day. I know Bubby would be proud!

To my sister, Lindsay, who has believed in me always, even when I didn't believe in myself: You were always game when I wanted to redecorate your bedroom. Saman, thank you for loving her and being the brother I always kinda wanted.

To Jay Neal (and my Rainbow Company Youth Theatre family): You taught me how to roll paint, forced me to use a jigsaw, and showed me the endless possibilities to build something. I know you're up there smiling.

BARRY

To my mom and dad: Thank you for giving me a childhood filled with love and amazing memories, but especially for giving me the space and freedom to follow my heart even when it terrified you. I know I often went in different directions than you wanted me to, and it means so much to me that you are proud of me anyway.

THE BROWNSTONE BOYS

To our Brooklyn family: Thank you for keeping us laughing, even when a ceiling is caving in and we're on our phones too much. We love you, you're family.

To everyone following us on social media, from our very first follower (Hi, BedStuy grandma Clarice!) to those who join our little corner: We can't thank you enough. We are constantly inspired by the stories you share with us. Special shout-out to our friends in the designer and influencer community. You know who you are.

To Alison Fargis, our book agent: We admire your dedication to your authors, and we are so grateful and honored to be part of the Stonesong family.

To Caitlin Leffel, Amanda Englander, and our Union Square & Co. family: You made it much easier than we ever thought it would be. Thank you for your patience working with us as first-time authors. You made our words and our work shine.

Thank you to photographers Nick Glimenkis and Christian Torres and videographer Jonathan Harwood, for dealing with our long shoot days. We love seeing our projects through your very creative eyes. Thank you, Andy Taray, for your illustrations.

To our contractors, architects, specialists, sales and showroom reps, vendors, and brand partners: We have learned from each of you.

We have loved every second of collaborating with our clients to build their dream homes. Thank you for letting us be part of your journey. We always describe it as a roller coaster ride, but we would go around with each of you again!

Kerri, Ryan, Erin, Haley, Alaina, and Rachel: We should really change our name to the Brownstone Squad, 'cause we can't do it without each of you! Thank you for indulging our crazy and being with us every step of the way on the daily drama called renovating.

To our management team at Parker and IKONICFOX: Thank you for stretching us when we have impostor syndrome and being a constant support. We love y'all.

To our baby, Zuko: Thank you for giving us two or three minutes between ball throws to write this book. And for the snuggles.

To *Sesame Street*: Thank you for educating us from an early age, and for our first introduction to a brownstone community.

Index

Photo Credits